Born into a family of potters and apprenticed at 17, Duncan's factory closed following the Suez catastrophe. He plunged into medicine at Edinburgh. This slice of memoir follows the overconfident young man through a rougher education in managing travel disasters and coping with crises.

To the future of Scottish tourism; may the early buds of whose flowering sketched in this story, fully justify the hopes of those whose vision is a business harvest mighty enough to contribute significantly to the economy of a free-standing state.

To the bus drivers and tourist guides of the last century; may their hard work for so little recognition eventually bring prosperity to their grandchildren.

To those many poor misguided souls, eager to do the right thing, who so often got things wrong; may they, too, be consoled to know that they have a very small place in the history of Scottish tourism, for, as TS Eliot wrote: *history is here and now*, or as he might have put it: *history is there and then*.

John A. T. Duncan

NOTHING CAN POSSIBLY GO WRONG

A Penny for the Guide

AUSTIN MACAULEY PUBLISHERS®

LONDON * CAMBRIDGE * NEW YORK * SHARJAH

A CIP catalogue record for this title is available from the British Library.

ISBN 9781035885848 (Paperback)
ISBN 9781035885855 (ePub e-book)

www.austinmacauley.com

First Published 2025
Austin Macauley Publishers Ltd®
1 Canada Square
Canary Wharf
London
E14 5AA

My warmest thanks to Duncan Lockerbie of Lumphanan Press, who first laid out this book for easy reading.

Also to Ritchie Collins for permission to use his picture *"Autumn Tower"*.

Introduction

Tour guiding is a well-established part of the entertainment profession. Its practitioners have shifted over the centuries from performers in street theatre to acting as companions for young aristocrats viewing the antiquities and brothels of the ancient world. Moving with the years, they were to be found offering themselves as guides to tourists of only modest means in all capital cities of the world. Latterly, i.e., for the last 150 years, Thomas Cook & Co. has employed thousands of them and with the mantle of his name, dignified their place in the travel industry. For all that, entertainment was and remains the key to getting a smiling client and a good tip.

Tour guides in 1950's Edinburgh may be said to have come in roughly four main varieties: firstly, those self-obsessed but temporarily unemployed actors who knew everything [in 1957, even Edinburgh had five live theatres], but who, in the great medieval tradition, were plainly making it up as they went along; secondly, those who, like the weary warrior guardians of ancient monuments, only repeated what they read in their written script and who would not be lured beyond it by questions; thirdly, the professionals, people who have been known in the great cities of Europe from time immemorial. They lived off their tips and recognised their occupation as being just another form of show business.

Fourth and finally, came those innocents, like me, who knew nothing, but were eager to improve. Those fresh and callow undergraduates who had the urge to travel but lacked the means were best advised to look for work with the many tour bus companies. For them, a good driver was essential. The driver-guide relationship resembled that between a ward sister and a houseman: only a stupid junior doctor would upset the ward sister. If the driver avoids a certain route or destination, there will usually be a good reason. For example, if he [60 years ago, drivers were all he] coughed hard in the middle of the guide's schtick, it meant 'stop; skip that one'. Those good, friendly drivers of sixty years ago were mostly in late middle age and utterly reliable. They made good avuncular tutors for their green as grass student guides.

A Student on the Tour Buses

Guiding on tour buses was essentially seasonal work and the demand for them happily coincided with the long vacation in the British university calendar. Good things in life frequently just drop unbidden at the recipient's feet. So, it was with me as a medical student in Edinburgh. I was trying to buy some textbooks from a fourth-year student who was a bit of an organiser. A product of some English public school, he just felt compelled to be at the heart of everything, the British Medical Students Association, the SRC[Students Representative Council], the Scottish Union of Students and by delegation, its SUS Travel Bureau. He was trying to find a last-minute replacement for a town tour the following afternoon. This was a chore that he, at the last minute, found inconvenient to perform himself, a lesson to him that being Mr Fixit had its downside. We struck a bargain involving books and a tour of Edinburgh. I had become a guide for the Scottish Union of Students' Travel Bureau.

In the 1950s, tour guides in Edinburgh often produced a rather disjointed catalogue of facts and characters, running: James IV [who the heck was he?], Mary Queen of Scots, James VI & 1st, Bonny Prince Charlie, Burke & Hare, Old Town and New Town. It had not yet dawned upon the native

Scots that they themselves had only a slender and disjointed knowledge of Scottish history, while visitors from overseas knew nothing at all.

History was taught in a confusing patchwork of colourful episodes in the primary schools of the fifties, probably because it was regarded as a relatively unimportant subject. Starting in 1707 with The Act of Union, Scottish became British history, full of flags and banners and victories. The odd primary teacher might have a fixation on nationalism, but that generally extended no further than Bannockburn and Bonnie Prince Charlie. For all that, tourists expected to be treated to the romantic but distressing stories of Mary, Queen of Scots and Bonnie Prince Charlie. They were not stupid and some of them were deeply well-informed, but few of them gained anything more from the tour guides' narrative of tribal treachery and regicide than an impression of a small country with an unimportant past.

The student guide was, therefore, faced with the necessity to do some reading of Scots history, extending far beyond the brief summaries on shortbread tins. Concise reliable books were very few indeed and none could bridge the gap between the ragged clans that fought at Bannockburn and the splendid eighteenth-century city that our tourists had paid to see. At this point, the serious guide had to strike a compromise between amusing the tourists and instructing them. This latter alternative was patronising and therefore, inappropriate, so the first choice had to be for a few comic or grotesque stories. Well chosen, they could do more than provide the string on which were displayed the pearls of architecture or sights of significance: a good story provides a peg on which to hang the memory of an enjoyable tour and clinging to that memory there will be at least one notable fact.

As a rank outsider and amateur, I felt that these tours of the city would benefit from a little dusting and polishing. With all the arrogance of youth, I drew up an itinerary for the bus driver to follow, starting from George Square, passing Greyfriars Kirk and the statue of the dog, Bobby, going across George IV Bridge, up the Lawn market to the castle esplanade and then down the Royal Mile to Holyrood House. The New Town would have to be a separate item.

On viewing my effort, Jock Peggie, my driver, was very unimpressed. He seemed to me to be ancient with his face brown and lined from constant exposure to the glare of day behind the panoramic windscreen of his bus. Probably he was only mid-fifties, but he was a widower who had three pleasures in life: bus driving, smoking and an evening dram [or two]. It was he who introduced me to 'Doch & Doruis', a couple whose charm does not fade with the years.

Jock Peggie looked at my proposed tours and growled, "John, you are far too serious. Remember these folks are on holiday. The tourists want a quick look around the town. They'll save their legs for shopping. Your tour is exactly the same as the standard city tour, and mind, they want it done in an hour, or hour and a half at the most. If you want to be different, we could take them along Princes Street and show them St Cuthbert's Burying Ground with its guard houses against body snatchers.

"Then tell them about Burke and Hare and we can go through the Grassmarket and do the creepy bits of Victoria street and the caves under George IV Bridge. Tell them that Greyfriars church yard was used as a concentration camp during the civil war. Drop them outside the pub. They will take photos of Greyfriars Bobby's statue and then go in for a drink. That's a good way to end a tour."

That was the best advice I ever received on guiding in Edinburgh.

Nearly all students of the fifties and sixties viewed vacations as an opportunity to earn money, to hitch hike through France or to do adventurous things, such as sail a yacht around the British Isles. Preclinical medical students were no use to hospital wards, whereas clinical students, by contrast, were obliged to build up a record of useful service in the hospital wards. The vacations in the preclinical years were the final burst of alternative life for medical students. More than that, the long vacation was a three-month opportunity to earn money at some unskilled routine job in industry or agriculture in order to supplement a grant that was intended to cover the thirty weeks of term time.

Having spent six years of my youth in the pottery industry, there was no point in wasting valuable recreational time working in a repetitive or low-paid job for a mere pittance. Tour guiding offered to broaden my parochial horizons with travel. Above all, Edinburgh touring offered me an introduction to this rare and for an Englishman, unapproachable beauty that was Scotland in 1958. The tour guide might earn a mere pittance, but he lived free of charge, often in places that he could not have afforded for himself. The job seemed worthwhile even to me, a penniless medical student; damn the money!

For medical students in the fourth, fifth and final years, the vacations had to be devoted to helping out in the hospital wards as clinical clerks. The clinical clerk was an odd phrase, a leftover from Victorian times. It meant anything from odd job man to locum house officer and was the only way to get onto the list of possibles for a house job in that particular unit after graduation. Those who neglected to 'show an interest' in clerkships could end up spending the summer after graduation applying for house officer posts in the North of England, where the hospitals were notoriously back woods institutions.

Touring Begins

It took very little intelligence [and I had a limited amount] to understand why my Fixit friend wanted to get out of the trip that was to be my introduction to tour guiding. The tourists were all French academics and spoke very little English. Luckily, my schoolboy command of French was still good enough to conduct thirty Francophones on a tour round Edinburgh and then continue, the next day, to the Trossachs, that green belt of hills and lochs that lies like a beautiful carpet at the entrance to the Highlands proper.

Fortunately, there was no need, the following afternoon, to translate the driver's angry comments when, on an unscheduled diversion onto a minor road, the bus grounded its belly on a hump-back bridge and stuck. Jock had not wanted to use this route precisely because of this bridge with its sharply rounded crest. He was furious but composed enough to summon help from a garage in nearby Callander. Meanwhile, it was enough to ask everyone to get off to lighten the load and to allow the bus to tear off exhaust pipes and various non-essential bits and pieces as it was hauled free of the bridge.

The bright side of this episode was owed to the fact that an inn, 'The Bailie Nicol Jarvie', stood immediately nearby.

Walter Scott's story of how Bailie Jarvie had set fire to a highlander's kilt with a red-hot poker was a good enough excuse for a glass of whisky. Warmed by the log fire and a dram or two, the male French tourists, eager students of applied alcohol, consulted the barman on his recommendations from a range of at least forty bottles. Their wives sensibly settled in front of the blazing logs for tea and shortbread. This outing was recorded as a success and the temporary guide was passed as OK, probably useable next season.

Crichton Street

The Scottish Union of Students' Travel Agency [SUS for short], rented from the university an office just off George Square in Crichton Street. The office occupied the ground floor of a rather down-at-heel stone-built house. It was early Georgian, like the whole of George Square into which its cobbled street flowed, but not nearly as decorative as its neighbours whose windows looked onto the lawns and trees in the centre of the square. These houses in the Square were built of roughly dressed ashlar in stones carefully placed in alternating colours of red and cream sandstone, giving their frontages a chequered, perhaps, dare one say, even a tartan pattern. Obviously, these houses when they were built were a cut or two above the average.

Crowded together on the west side of the Square, the houses formed a terrace. The plaques on their walls still parade the names of famous writers who had spent their youth at this or that address, people like Walter Scott and Conan Doyle [No. 22c]. These houses alone escaped the savage 'modernisation' of the university area.

That dusty antique house sheltering the Students' Travel Bureau, together with three-quarters of George Square was later to be vandalised, torn down by an ancient university to make way for its first wave of functional but inadequate concrete boxes in an aspiration to modernity, whatever that might mean.

Three permanent staff, all lady graduates in law, ran this all-season highly specialised travel bureau and had succeeded in capturing a lot of academic business in the UK and abroad. They had discovered a niche market but were too small to wield any commercial clout. Somehow or other, these three managed to squeeze a viable business out of various airlines offering especially cheap charter flights [mostly at unpopular hours, such as 5 am] and the various European railways that lured students onto their less used routes. Between them, they wrung special student deals from the smaller private hotels of Edinburgh and cajoled various universities into making their halls of residence available [at a suitable price] to SUS tours.

As instant communication was still thirty years in the future, their business was fraught with delay and uncertainty and so was very stressful. Bearing this in mind, it needs to surprise none of us that the travel business has ruined so many agencies both large and small.

I went to Crichton Street to try to capitalise on my success with the French bus party. The office manager, Esme Walker, a sweet-faced, neat little woman in her mid-twenties and just married to another law student sat behind a table untidily strewn with papers and travel time tables. Two telephones stood at her elbow, a large typewriter sat sullenly in front of her. Versatility was obviously the name of her game. What does one call such a woman? Joan of all trades sounds wrong, while Superwoman exaggerates.

"Call me Esme," she said, so solving my puzzle. "This is Mireille Gateau, my deputy."

They were persuaded by my success with the French tourists that they needed somebody like me, an experienced traveller, fluent in French and a practitioner of barrack room German. I did not expect to hear any more from them until the following spring, so I should have guessed that something was amiss when my friend, Fixit, showed up one stormy winter evening in early December. There had been an administrative cock up [nothing to do with him, of course]. The agency had booked a particularly long winter tour for twenty US students to travel round several cities of Western Europe during the Christmas vacation, and they had not secured the services of enough guides.

The agency was on the point of curtailing the expedition. They were desperate for just such a person as I had painted myself to be to take this mixed party of twenty US students to Austria, Italy and Bavaria during the Christmas vacation. The whole tour, sixteen women and four men, was to be conducted by train and I was to join them in Salzburg, where I would relieve another guide with whom the tourists would have 'done' Amsterdam, Cologne and Salzburg. It seemed like a plumb job. Nothing could possibly go wrong.

Armed only with a large Manilla envelope containing my itinerary, a letter of introduction to various hotel managements, and a large yellow piece of paper masquerading as an International Railway Travel warrant, naming me and my party of twenty, I set off from a cold and frosty Waverley Station in late December. It was a long journey to Salzburg. After spending the night with friends near London, I caught an express to Dover and boarded a twin-funnel British Rail channel ferry.

The best way to cross the channel by steamer was to sit in the dining room and have a meal. In those days, the ferries had a large dining room where waiters in black ties served excellent hot meals to travellers sitting at tables set with white table cloths and white linen napkins. It was an excellent way to spend the 180-minute crossing, therapeutic, even, as the constant swallowing helped to settle the traveller's queasy stomach.

At Calais the train to Paris Nord awaited, connecting with trains from Gare de L'Orient, the transcontinental probing by night through Switzerland to Austria. It took me twenty hours to reach Salzburg, travelling third class. No sleeper ticket was included in the bunch of papers handed to me in Edinburgh. Awaiting my arrival in Salzburg was Alan, a final-year medic, who was, to put it mildly, eager to part company with his charges. After handing over a large envelope filled with itineraries and tickets, he suggested that we retreat to a nearby bistro for a meal and a drink.

Only when I had lost the pallor of my overnight train journey, did he reveal the jagged bleeding truth.

"The men are OK, but four of the women are a bloody nightmare. You won't believe how stupid they are. They stick together like a bunch of mussels on a rope and yet they seem to believe that they're irresistibly attractive to European men. One silly bitch, in particular, is going to give you a wheelbarrow full of trouble because she has lost her passport and all her money. She was chatted up and charmed by some gigolo on the train coming here. He took her shopping in Salzburg city centre. Outside an expensive dress shop, he said that he felt stupid going in among women's clothes and that he would stay outside with her baggage; this included a massive shoulder bag with her money and passport.

"When she came out of the store, he had gone, evaporated, skedaddled. I've been with her to the American consul here in Salzburg and he informs me that an emergency passport will be supplied in ten days' time, so I think you will have to pick her up here on your way back from Italy. The consul will take care of her meanwhile. Believe me, she's poisonous and if she ever had a sense of humour, there's no trace of it now.

"Oh, I should have mentioned it earlier. You are taking the night express to Florence tonight at eleven o' clock. The SUS budget didn't run to sleepers, so it will be another all-night journey on your bum."

Alan, the lucky fellow, was heading next for a skiing holiday in the Tyrol, so I walked with him to the main railway station. Then I was alone in a strange city wrapped in the false twilight of the street lamps. Salzburg, no doubt, can look very Christmassy in the snow, but there was no snow. Darkness and a steady drizzle stretched before me as an unwanted part of my six hours wait. Luckily, this was Salzburg and not Edinburgh. German and Austrian pubs are very good about providing plenty of newspapers for their patrons to read, so I spent the rest of the evening drinking coffee, eating sausages and deciphering the newspapers before wearily slinging my bag over to the main railway station.

My party of young American students was easy to locate as they grouped themselves in a circle to ward off any hostile natives or Red Indians. Anxious to be prepared for the inevitable rush for seats when the barrier gates were opened to the international platform, I took a roll call, duly noting the absence of one US woman. The seats were all in one carriage but in four different compartments. Several women declared that they wanted a bed in the sleeper section and were willing to pay. With twenty minutes to go before the train departed, I felt that this request should have received attention a little earlier, say, twenty-four hours earlier.

Always willing, I found the guard for the sleeper and asked about the possibility of buying tickets for the sleeper at this late stage. The man laughed at me and said quite pleasantly that it was too late and would have been too late four days ago; that this was an international train and not a local train people take casually and that Christmas is one of the high points of traveller movement, and that the ski season was just starting. I had already guessed the latter fact from the special ski racks lining the corridors of Austrian trains.

My female travellers, before distributing themselves into their reserved seats, let me understand that their opinion of my negotiating skills was low. I reserved my own comments on their forward-planning skills, but they had a valid point. An all-night journey in the upright sitting position is not only tedious; it's bloody uncomfortable.

Florence

We arrived, after a journey of fifteen hours, in one of the most beautiful cities I had ever seen. A hotel porter met us on arrival; indeed, several hotel porters from other establishments were waiting on the platform. Their competition for customers was loud and intense. Room prices, half board rates, full board rates, all were rolling and clattering upon us as though they were skittles in a bowling alley. Our modest hotel was warm and we were all eager to have an early supper before settling down to catch up with a lost night's sleep.

Walking through the stone slab streets of Florence as we followed the hotel porter in the dusk of a wet afternoon was enough to sharpen my awareness that this city was something special. The window displays in themselves were a delight and my memory retains a vivid image of a scarlet silk high-heeled shoe that stood all alone, highlighted against a background of black velvet with absolutely nothing else to distract the attention of those passing in the street.

I knew what I wanted to see, but the American women were determined to go shopping for silver and any other loot that their dollars could buy. The four men, on the other hand, were more interested in seeing the Duomo and the Medici

Tombs and the art gallery; yet, willy nilly, we all had to pass through the many booths of silver smiths on the Ponte Vecchio to get to the Uffizi Art Gallery.

Not surprisingly, the Medici Tombs reminded me of the architecture of the New Quadrangle in Edinburgh Medical School, but Florence was a city as distinctively different among the cities of the world as that red silk shoe was different from an army boot. For all that, Edinburgh and Florence could claim some kinship. It rained in Florence so often that it had long become the centre of the Italian umbrella industry. Street traders loaned out for a small fee, umbrellas which were discarded in the streets of the city after use.

Florence in the winter still belonged to its citizens. Their domestic links reached out into the surrounding valleys and mountains. This community was much more than a set of shopkeepers and hoteliers. In the middle of a small square near the Ponte Vecchio, there stood an old man playing the bag pipes. He was dressed in a rough sheepskin and looked very down-at-heel. People told me that he was playing the Umbrian pipes, though they looked just like the medieval pipes in the hands of the stone angel carved in Rosslyn Chapel. Sympathetic onlookers said that times were very bad for the farmers in the mountains. I put a few coins in his hat.

Rome

The first thing that strikes the traveller on arrival at Rome's main station is the beauty of the modern architecture. Never before had I seen concrete buildings in any form other than that of lifeless rectangular boxes, but these structures swooped, curved and flowed in cascades. They were the very opposite of the rough utilitarian stuff of post-war Britain.

To get to our hotel, wherever that may be, we had to rely on taxis, of which there were plenty, too many, in fact. I discovered rather late that it was better to take a city cab from the front of the station because they all have meters. Unfortunately, I had shepherded my flock through a side door and straight into the waiting private or pirate taxis. Four taxis were needed and I had negotiated terms with two drivers while another portion of my group did their own thing and took off in two more.

We arrived on the Via Nomentana, a fairly central, broad, tree-lined street to find a heated row in full progress between one of the male students and a taxi driver. Joe was from New Jersey and spoke fluent Italian. He was telling the driver that his charge was excessive and held out a handful of coins in payment, but obviously not in full payment. The driver angrily knocked the coins onto the pavement. Things could have got worse had this driver not found himself outnumbered by our arrival. He decided to withdraw, but just for good luck, he spat heavily upon the fallen coins. Joe just left them in the street and walked off into the guest house where we were to stay.

Many of the women students were Catholics and so was Joe. Two of them had wangled an introduction from their local bishop to the Papal Chamberlain and were foolishly hoping for an audience at this busy time in the Christian calendar, with the new Pope John. They also wrongly assumed that midnight Mass in St Peters on Christmas Eve would be free to all comers. Unfortunately, it was, as usual, confined to the diplomatic service and senior churchmen. I was not much given to churchgoing nor nostalgia but by great good luck, the US consul recommended the American Protestant Church in Rome for our midnight service on Christmas Eve and mentioned a suitable restaurant for a traditional turkey dinner.

I fancied that this was a considerable coup; a success for their British guide. It was not to prove so. The three wicked witches, though they ate the turkey, complained that what they received was a Thanksgiving Dinner!

As I mentioned earlier, I was not then, and am not now, a religious person. The various religions of the world have, over the centuries, been responsible for just as much mayhem and mass murder as Stalin, Mao and Hitler lumped together. Given my scepticism, I was surprised by respect for the new Pope John in 1958.

My whole group joined thousands of others in St Peter's Square at eleven on Christmas morning. High above the crowd on a wide balcony, the papal band played through its repertoire, not once or twice, but again and again. At half past eleven, the Pope still had not appeared and a general muttering began among the assembled crowd, 'Where was the old guy? Had he slept over after officiating at midnight Mass for the high and mighty? It was bloody rude to keep the faithful waiting in the freezing cold.'

Actually, the weather was so mild in Rome that I did not bother to wear a coat, but I had to admit that the papal band was getting ragged and playing a little indistinctly by eleven forty. Then news began to filter through the crowd, like smoke blown by the wind. It appeared that Pope John had celebrated Mass at a large prison at six and again at eight at a large hospital. It was thought that he was just coming back from a very poor part of Rome, where he had also conducted Mass. From these locations, even I could piece together St Matthew's homily.

"I was sick and ye visited me: I was in prison, and ye came unto me."

Just before twelve, a chauffeur-driven battered old Lancia limousine with its rear roof of crumpled old black leather folded down drove up to the great portico. A dumpy figure got out and scuttled into St Peters, appearing more or less on the last stroke of twelve on the balcony beside the exhausted band. The usual papal blessing tumbled through a sometimes crackling, sometimes booming, sometimes shrieking PA system that had seen much better days in its youth. The crowd did not know quite what to make of this Pope and his Christmas Day show; their enthusiasm for this new low-key old man was muted and unsure. Two days later, we moved on to Venice.

As another long overnight train journey stared at me from my sheaf of tickets, I spent an hour or two at the central railway station to buy an upgrade to Wagons Lit. The students had all agreed to kick in the extra money required and the sleeper space was available. The only difficult bit lay in finding the right Italian words to match my requirements. The obvious solution was to stand in line behind other people booking sleeper accommodation. When I got too near to the ticket window and if I still felt insecure, I would yield my place to the person behind me, "Prego; scusi."

Slowly, the necessary vocabulary was accumulated from eavesdropping the words used by the persons in front of me at the window. It worked well enough to keep my American critics quiet if not happy. They remained sceptical of my competence throughout and held firmly to the belief that foreigners and Europeans could not be trusted.

Venice in Winter

We arrived at Venice Central Station to be greeted by the same scrum of hotel porters as at Florence and Rome. As expected, a porter from the large pensione into which we had been booked took possession of us and led us to a quayside facing a large expanse of turquoise water. Our view of Venice was limited by a freezing fog which added a strangely attractive sparkle to the mysterious scene as our hotel porter bundled us onto a large green public water bus. The shining brass handrails of the ferry pointed us across the water to a looming grey mass, about 500 metres away. This mass gradually transformed into a handsome church with a dome and an adjacent red sandstone lantern tower. This was Santa Maria Della Salute; our pensione hid quietly in its shadow.

Venice in its winter clothing was a city quite different from the summer tourist attraction. This strange city of canals and footpaths looked quite genteel in its foggy tweeds. In the absence of crowds of tourists, movement around the centre was easy and prices in the coffee houses and restaurants had become affordable to the long-term residents, few of whom were princes or millionaires.

Only a few of the major tourist attractions were open to visitors in the winter of 1958/9, so we looked at the Doge's

Palace, the Bridge of Sighs and St Mark's Cathedral. The Campanile looked like too much climbing and, anyway, who wanted to look at the view when it was wrapped in dense fog?

My old friend, Tim Showan, who had once held an Italian travelling scholarship in art had long ago been enthusiastic about the Biennale Art Exhibitions in Venice, so that was where I went on the second morning. It was a seminal experience to see Byzantine art, glowing with scarlet and gold, exhibited so starkly, the naked canvases being stripped of elaborate frames and hung on walls of plain sackcloth. By this device, the visitor was freed from the distraction of fussy frames and forced to focus on the painting itself. For a young man from the Potteries, this was an extraordinary discovery.

During our brief visit to Venice, I managed to get a box for ten in the opera house for an afternoon performance of 'The Barber of Seville.' The limited number made no difference as most of the women wanted to go shopping for Murano glass at the factory. The Mozartian Venice opera house was rather small and possibly deliberately so, considering that it dated back some 200 years to a time when there would be no sound amplifiers and the singer's voice might struggle to get up to the top of the house. Three circles of rather dusty gilding rose above a small stage and the whole effect was one of diminished gentility. My companions mostly found the whole experience delightful but would have preferred the movies.

When we departed for Vienna on 30 December on another long train journey, I discovered that yet another US woman was missing from the roll call. The women knew all about this, but nobody had thought to tell me. Their attitude towards me alternated strangely between regarding me as the hired hand to be booted, or as the figure of authority to be defied. The woman in question had met up, by arrangement, with her boyfriend in the USAF, who was stationed somewhere in Italy. The word was that they were taking an early honeymoon and that she would rejoin the party in Munich for the last leg of the journey home. Thanks, a bleeding bundle for letting me know!

Vienna for New Year

Immediately after the war, Vienna had been divided into four administrative areas: French, British, Russian and American. This occupation had ended with the signing of an official peace treaty in 1955, but, as with the arrangement in Germany, the American forces had withdrawn to a few strategic bases rather than leave an unprotected Austria to its own devices. For many of us, Vienna conjured up black-and-white cinema images of the grim occupied city of 'The Third Man.' It was a place of mystery and danger with somebody plonking away on a zither to provide background music. It turned out to be a rather different place for us in 1958.

Vienna was cold but the winter snow was slow in coming. Joe and I shared a room in a guest house. We not only had our own adjoining bathroom, but our accommodation contained a giant green tiled stove for heating the room and our bath water. As we were out sightseeing all day, our bath water was never hot enough to use. A porter delivered breakfast for two to our door every morning. It was always four crisp rolls, butter, jam and coffee with plenty of hot milk. I liked it but Joe longed for corn flakes and orange juice.

Joe was a curious fellow, very likeable and highly intelligent, but struggling to come to terms with his Italian

Catholic mother's wish for him to become a priest. He looked a bit like 'Popeye' in the Hollywood film 'The French Connection'; same square figure, just below middle height, the same pork pie hat, same well-worn black coat. He could have been a New York cop, or a crook, or a candidate for holy orders.

While we were in Rome, he had been to visit the seminary for US students training for the priesthood. Something about his visit had disturbed him, I don't know what, but he started long conversations over coffee, about the meaning of life and the place of religion in society. He was thinking of switching to business studies. I often wonder what became of him back in the USA.

Our guest house was in the suburbs, but still very close to the Ringbahn, the ancient but excellent metropolitan tramway that circled and quartered the city. For a very small fare, it would take us anywhere: the Royal Palace, the State Art Gallery, the giant Ferris Wheel; the city was at the disposal of its visitors. As students, we all carried special IDs that gave us free entry into museums, cathedrals and palaces, so we visited Schoenbrunn palace, the State Art Gallery and St Stephens Cathedral. The giant Ferris Wheel charged a substantial fee, so we left that for well-off visitors to Vienna.

The State Art Gallery was so incredibly well endowed with the treasures of a long-gone empire that the visitor was forced to recognise that the Hapsburgs had once been rich beyond reckoning. Their possessions had spanned the greater part of South America and Western Europe. They were the kingpins, the team to beat, right up to 1870. Their Imperial art gallery contained, not one or two paintings by Velasquez, but two large rooms full of his masterpieces. It was the same for most of the European painters of the sixteenth, seventeenth and eighteenth centuries. It seemed like looking at the treasures of Tutankhamen's tomb; a rich mausoleum with no present-day connections.

Vienna's Ring district, the equivalent of Britain's Westminster, contained the ministerial buildings in a rather vulgar mid-nineteenth-century style, all depicting gigantic mythical war gods or bearded soldiers with huge hats. Despite this architectural essay in arrogant military self-assertion, there was no denying that Vienna had an old-time charm. Ignoring two world wars and two foreign invasions, Vienna's clocks seemed to have been stopped in 1914. Tourists, crowded its many eating places, eager to eat Linzer Torte, Sacher Torte or schnitzel, and then to gaze at the remains of Imperial glory. It has to be admitted that the Viennese pubs and restaurants with their warmth and friendly atmosphere were very affordable in 1958 and very attractive.

Some of the women students had brought ball gowns in their luggage, expecting to attend the Vienna Opera's New Year Ball. It was disappointing to be the bearer of the sad news that this ball was and is the main annual event of Viennese high society and that tickets are always sold out about a year in advance. There were, of course, alternative New Year attractions, but our disappointed Cinderellas preferred to seek solace in a rather sleek restaurant. Joe and I discretely left them at 23.30 in order to join the crowds letting in New Year outside St Stephen's Cathedral.

High up, on a balcony above the crowds thronging the square in front of the Cathedral, a white-clad choir sang a selection of carols and hymns. It was almost perfectly charming, but once again, as at St Peters in Rome, the PA system spoiled the occasion by failing altogether. Sound did not carry well on frosty air; it floated down from a great height, indistinct and scattered like a cloud of feathers. Many in the crowd were restless as they waited in the cold night and one could understand without approving the bad behaviour of groups of youths who whistled and shouted ribaldries. Things, however, threatened to take an ugly turn when some of these youngsters started to throw fireworks into the crowd.

One such youth stood in the crowd, only a few yards from me. Without any preamble, a middle-aged man just grabbed him and slapped him around the face, once, twice, three times. It occurred to me that this man was quite old enough to have served in the Wehrmacht and he certainly had about him all the bearing of an army NCO. The chastised youth and his companions just crept away as the crowd applauded the ex-sergeant. I doubted then and I still doubt now that any such sensible disciplinarian would have emerged in a British crowd. We are a timid kind of people who tend to avoid that sort of trouble and who, consequently, tolerate bottle-throwing hooligans in Hogmanay crowds.

At the midnight hour, the clock in one of the two Gothic gables fronting St Stephens went through its introductory rattle of chimes and then struck firmly twelve times. The choir sang a short anthem and the show was over. People in the crowd shook hands and turned to go their various ways. Joe and I decided to let the crowd melt a little before we tried to board a tramcar back to our suburban guest house. We dodged more or less at random into a well-lit inn, just off St Stephen's Square.

The warmth of the series of small rooms was immediately matched by the warmth of our welcome from a sturdy inn keeper who looked like a character out of an Ealing Films production of Pickwick Papers. He herded us gently into one of a series of six-person cubicles, formed by a narrow table with, on either side, a high-back wooden settle. On the reverse of each settle was a series of coat hooks, for this was an inn in a city well accustomed to winter weather. To our surprise and delight, our host produced out of nowhere a large jug full of hot 'gluhwein'; not only this, but he also produced four of our young women students and slotted them with us into our little cubicle. The evening progressed from there from pleasant to truly memorable.

New Year's Day brought the first flurries of snow, just gentle hints of worse yet to come. Joe's Popeye hat now looked less eccentric, so I cast around the market stalls in one of the central squares. A brisk trade was being carried on in lucky golden pig coins; in warm wine and gingerbread; in hot sausages and floury rolls; in ribbons and silks and colourful cottons, but no hats. Then I found what I needed right in the middle of the market place. There a large stall stood as though in a country fair, loaded with Alpenstocks and walking sticks, with leather goods and gloves, with woollen sweaters and scarves, and, of course, with Tyrolean hats.

A charming stall holder, with blue eyes and blond hair wound in plaits round her head helped me to choose my hat, coaxing me with a mirror into believing myself to be a truly handsome young man. Reluctant to just break away, I allowed her to sell me some silver edelweiss to wear in my hat, just like a Tyrolean farmer. Joe also thought that the silver badges for his hat were a good idea, though I think it was the blue eyes and blond plaits that really interested him.

I had promised the students to inquire about the possibility of tickets for the New Year's Day Strauss concert. Once again, these tickets were sold out months in advance, but the box office suggested that students sometimes could get special seats at the opera on the day of a performance. This information turned out to be both good and bad. The good bit was that there would be standing places for students at the rear of the dress circle. The bad bit was that these places would not be sold until six-thirty and the opera started at seven. Interest in this idea was zero, even Joe crossed himself in fear of a Beethoven opera. A small group of us spent the afternoon walking in the Vienna woods.

Just to be sure of getting a place, even a standing place, for 'Fidelio' at the Vienna State Opera, I turned up at five. I was not alone. About twenty people stood in a small passage to the right of the box office, some of them evidently hoping for returned tickets. Ticket prices were outrageous by Edinburgh standards, but by six-thirty, no returns had been offered and quite suddenly I found only six people in front of me. Using a student card, my standing place cost me about one pound.

For a trivial sum, I was admitted, hat and all, to the world's leading opera house and one of life's most special experiences: 'Fidelio' sung by some of the world's greatest singers and played by one of the world's greatest orchestras. It is a long opera and in this great opera house there were many bars, but this was a 'white tie' occasion and none would allow in a scruff like me. There was nowhere for me even to leave my coat and hat. The standing place was behind the dress circle, in itself an exalted position, to be sure, but to see anything one had to stand on a step behind a wooden partition about 1.5m tall with a brass rail on top as a hand grip for weary students. I remember very little of the magnificence of the opera house itself, but the memory of 'Fidelio' endures.

The queen of the great shopping bag heist turned up at our humble guest house in the suburbs of Vienna, having spent fourteen days at a five-star hotel, the bill for which was paid eventually by her parents. As charming as ever, she spoke only to her three female buddies to convey to me that she would meet us all under the clock at the Hauptbahnhof the following morning when the tour moved on to Munich. Joe politely enquired about the health of her passport, only to receive a squirt of verbal impurities not commonly used among ladies of a genteel persuasion.

Munich

Our departure from Vienna was early morning; three large taxis had been arranged to take us to the station. I hoped that Lady Macbeth would be on time because I now had to worry about the young woman who had gone off for an informal honeymoon with her USAF lover. She had left a telephone message for me with the proprietrix of the guest house, assuring me that she would be on the platform at 6 am but I was uneasy with all this informality, which seemed to me more like sheer bloody rudeness.

They say that history repeats itself as farce and here was Miss Lovenest bringing me her own ridiculous story. She too had lost her passport; must have packed it in with her lover's baggage. The USAF flyboy was now on an airfield somewhere in Northern Italy, too far away to be of immediate help. With the train due to leave in fifteen minutes, there was no alternative to just trusting luck that passport controls on the train could be avoided.

Munich was to be a brief twelve-hour stopover before we caught yet another night train; this time to the Ostend Ferry. It was a city of clamorous modern glass and concrete, side by side with buildings of great antique charm. It seemed to be doggedly devoted to sweeping away the detritus of war, while preserving those relics of the past that dug deep, beyond mere sentimentality, into their civic self-image. Yet another open-air winter market was busily selling hot wine and golden pig coins, but the falling snow was getting thicker by the hour, so we retired into the Frauenkirche Dohm, the cathedral standing on guard by the central square.

Bavaria, of which Munich is the capital city, is a largely Catholic state and the women of my tour group were also of that belief. A German-speaking American nun, working as a tour guide for the Cathedral Church of Our Lady, quickly spotted my students and gently relieved me of my guide duty. I disentangled myself, leaving clear instructions for meeting again at eight in the evening. Freed of my charges, I made for the nearby Hofbrau Haus.

Night Train to Ostend

On entering this high Gothic Hall, panelled throughout with carved and fretted wood, there seemed to be a shadow at my elbow. It was Joe, looking more than ever like a Jersey tough guy. He said, "I can't take these women much longer. They wear their faith like the latest shade of lipstick."

Poor Joe! He really was serious about religion, but he wore his faith deep in his heart and felt offended by the way the young women in question waved Catholicism around like a Dior scarf. We sat in the warm glow of the Hofbrau Haus talking about the sort of philosophical questions that young men usually avoid. As the snow continued to bank itself into drifts, swept along by a wind that was slowly gathering blizzard strength, Joe and I drank beer and ate hot sausages and banged the long table in front of us in time to the Schrammel band, all unrealistically clad in lederhosen. When we finally left the beer hall to catch the midnight train, the band were also departing, this time dressed in snow boots and long sheepskin coats. Buzzing with beer and Yodel-eh-hi-hi, Joe and I slipped and staggered our way to the Hauptbahnhof.

Fuddle and fuzz was not a good defence against attack by the daughter of Chief Crazy Horse. She wanted blood and scalps in retribution for my neglect of Miss Lovenest. Her argument ignored the two facts governing the situation: that the missing passport was now in Italy and that its holder was two borders away in Germany. It added up to this: that Mr USAF, who [with military permission] could travel would have to bring the document personally to Miss Lovenest, who could not travel. The US Consul in Munich, a man who seemed to have greeted New Year rather too enthusiastically, had wearily explained that only the US Embassy in Bonn could issue a replacement document and that the process would require seven to ten days. He had pointedly locked his office after our meeting that afternoon.

All this was patiently explained to Miss Crazy Horse, whose reply was, "I suppose this appeals to your British sense of humour. You Brits, you just don't try hard enough. How much money have you offered the ticket collector to forget about her?"

From this, it looked as though the Daughter of Crazy Horse had been spreading it that one of our group lacked a passport. Things looked bad, even when viewed through a fuzzy pink fog. The non-sleeper carriages of the night train were divided up into the standard six or eight-person compartments, each side of which bore a large overhead luggage rack. The girls prepared a bed of coats on one such rack and proposed to hide Miss Lovenest there, suitably covered with light luggage. Joe said, "That's the first place they'll look. Go underneath the bench."

It was all a waste of time and effort. After an hour, the inevitable passport controllers appeared, unmistakeable in their long black leather coats and air of total detachment. They obviously knew perfectly well who it was who lacked a passport, just as I knew perfectly well that if I were to offer them a bribe, I would be taking my front teeth home in a match box. Absolutely no way would the young student be allowed to continue her journey. At an unscheduled halt by a lonely country platform, on a dark and snowy night, I pressed into her wet hands a wad of Deutchmarks, collected in my Tyrolean hat from the other students and said goodbye. A police car bore her away.

The train trundled on through the night, through dark and deserted stations, pausing briefly at Aachen before entering Belgium. Passengers were requested not to leave the train which would next stop at Ostend. A rather grumpy, dishevelled group of travellers reached London at five in the evening and split immediately into several groups, each going in a different direction. No goodbye greetings were exchanged and the guide's Tyrolean hat remained firmly on his head, empty of tips.

A few days later, the same guide reported to the untidy SUS Travel Bureau in Edinburgh. They had been informed of the series of passport losses and the measures taken to deal with them. This had been passed on to the originators of the tour in the USA. Surprisingly, SUS subsequently received private communication from their counterparts at Duke University, apologising for the 'totally irresponsible behaviour' of some of their female students. There was no problem and I could now get down to the bread and butter of guiding tourists around Edinburgh. It was laid down as policy by Bureau Chief Esme Walker that trips abroad had to be earned by weeks of tour guiding in Edinburgh and around Scotland.

What Was There to See
in Edinburgh?

The short answer was: one heck of a lot, and the best way to see most of it was on foot. In fact, in 1956, the best way to get to know any small area like central Edinburgh was by walking around it. Big cities, like Paris or Canberra, were simply too big to walk across in the morning, but Edinburgh was different. This strange city fascinated me from the moment I first arrived at the Caledonian Railway Station. It was a dark early evening in autumn. Street lamps along Princes Street sparkled in the light mist, like gentle fireworks at a children's party, while the lights of the passing traffic made the swirling scene glow with reds and yellows.

Edinburgh appealed to my youthful ardour. She seemed to be a beautiful woman with dark secrets in her past and I immediately wanted to know more about her. Interest, admiration and love followed in quick succession and I soon yearned to belong; at first to the city and then to Scotland. Like a cheeky young man sighting a beautiful young woman at a distance, I urgently wanted to get very close to her.

Once shorn of its suburbs, delightful though some of them may be, the central area splits like a peach into three portions, with Arthur's Seat rising like the fruit stone, separate, yet dominating both Old Town and New Town. The central portion around Arthur's Seat was my original area of exploration.

It seemed logical to start by exploring my immediate surroundings. At a time when most university students in Edinburgh lived at home and the total of university students of all sorts was about 7,000, I was lodged in Salisbury Green, one of only two university hostels for men. The great bulk of official accommodation was for women only, so I was privileged to get a room in this elderly Scottish Baronial mansion. It stood on several acres of its own grounds, poking its spiky turrets into the surrounding great elms. The enveloping grounds included another Scottish Baronial mansion, sinister in its spikes and stone cannons. This was the original St Trinians and I learned this on day one, when the First Year of Medicine had their mug shots taken with numbered cards held under our chin. On the back of my card was a school photograph taken in 1938, depicting the girls of St Trinians in front of the building that stood only 100 yards from Salisbury Green. The starchy lady headmistress was named in the picture as Miss Searle.

There could not have been a better place to start learning about this quirky city. Salisbury Green still stands on the Dalkeith Road, but now it is a smart, upmarket hotel operated by the university. The great expanse of grounds now houses about 3000 students in what is now known as The Pollock Halls of Residence and was gifted to the university by Sir Donald Pollock. The whole estate was originally the private residence of the Nelson family, whose larger printing factory stood opposite the owner's home.

The Nelsons must have made a fortune out of printing and publishing in the mid-nineteenth century and were proud to build two splendid houses to advertise their success. It was said that the founder of the firm stipulated to the builders that they should include in the roof works an exact copy of the cottage in which he was born. This enabled him to shut himself away from unwanted visitors with the excuse that he was 'away at his Highland cottage.'

Where the Commonwealth Olympic swimming pool now stands was, at the time of my residence in Salisbury Green, a beautiful green meadow, used as a sports field by the Nelson Print works. On this field, in the autumn and winter, the local amateurs played each other in the junior football league. In the summer, Saturday afternoon was reserved for cricket, but for most of the time, the field would be in the possession of the City of Edinburgh Police Pipe Band who would practice strenuously in their determination to retain the World Championship.

Pipe music stirs the soul of man, but it is best heard in concert. Practice tended to produce not so much music as cacophony when small groups of drummers and pipers were scattered all over Nelson's field, each group trying to perfect a different phrase of the music. Very much to the point was the fact that this racket carried on into the late evening; this at a time when all the students were reading hard to prepare for the end of year examinations. I wrote, as secretary of the house committee, on behalf of 50 students to ask the chief constable whether the band could cease practice at 7 pm. Of course, this request had to be wrapped in very diplomatic terms, stressing our collective love of pipe music, our admiration of the Police Pipe Band and our warmest best wishes for their success in the forthcoming championship. A very kindly chief constable wrote back, thanking us for our good wishes and transferring band practice to another field between a golf course and the Forth.

One of the first problems to confront a guide taking tourists around Edinburgh is the city centre's division into two main parts, as mentioned above. The guide, to fulfil the terms of a city tour, is forced into ignoring the many beautiful suburbs nursing the Royal Botanic Gardens, or the zoo, and wonderful villages, like Cramond or Duddingston or Swanston or Colinton, not to mention seaside promenades along the Forth at Portobello and Cramond.

In ninety minutes, the guide has to present a fairly indifferent audience with a potted history of Scotland as illustrated by selected buildings passing before them as their bus pursues its prescribed course over the cobbles of the Royal Mile and the tarmac of Princes Street. Mostly, in those days, the tourist ended up with a dog's breakfast of scraps of fact and morsels wrapped in gory details. The whole thing had to be contained in a woven basket of anecdotes. The better the guide's stories, the better the tourists' tips.

Holyrood Palace

Truth was an early casualty of such stories, yet it seemed scarcely to matter. Scots and non-Scots shared the same ignorance of Scotland's past, while sharing the same shavings that passed for knowledge, say, the story of Bruce and the spider. The shameful truth was that in 1958, Scottish history was widely regarded, even among educated Scots, as a boring story of internecine intrigue and murder, culminating in the Civil Wars which wasted almost the whole of the seventeenth century.

On any guided tour, this impression would be reinforced by a visit to the Palace of Holyrood House. The bloodstains, probably refreshed with red ink, on the floorboards of Mary Stuart's sitting room, reminded us that marital jealousy was not invented by Hollywood. Poor young Rizzio! His bloodstains form a better memorial than the one that his Queen awarded to his killer. Hands up who knows where there is a memorial to Darnley?

The official guides to Holyrood Palace were incredibly dull in the fifties. I guess the job may have been given to time-served army NCOs, as were the jobs in that other army establishment, Edinburgh Castle. Somebody should have told them, and obviously, somebody eventually did tell them, how little it added to the pleasure of the visit to hear them recite a long list of the names of the kings of Scotland as they trailed twenty tourists past twenty portraits of these same monarchs. It was, moreover, perfectly obvious that all these portraits were by the same artist and that he had used the same model throughout. Perhaps it was supposed to strengthen family likeness and legitimise the succession. The tour of the Royal apartments that followed this walk down the gallery of portraits left the impression of a rather moth-eaten holiday home. It's much better now.

The Castle

The castle was good value for money for the tourists if not for their guide. Once inside the ramparts, the professional army guides took over and they had an excellent line of patter and anecdotes. Even more to the point, these retired NCOs had a small field gun with which to fire off a blank for the one o'clock time signal. Children would cover their ears and scream at the explosion, while their parents would laugh as the gunner looked over the battlements before saying, 'Missed again!'

At the end of their tour, these worthies would stand collecting clinking coins from a happy and amused audience. The tour guide, who had no lines to speak in this bit of show business, got nothing.

With its small collection of the Scottish crown jewels, the castle modestly acknowledged that Scotland was smaller and poorer than its partner in the Union, but significantly different, another country quite separate in spirit from the shamefaced, bombastic England of 1956. I warmed to the castle all the more when I found the names of three members of our family in the Book of Remembrance in the War Memorial chapel. That great but silent prayer in stone has an altar grounded upon the naked rock at the highest part of the outcrop that runs down the High Street and the Royal Mile to the gates of the Palace of Holyrood House.

Symbolism abounded in the castle, from the small stone chapel of Queen Margaret who brought Christianity to Scotland, to the small high precipitous bedroom window from which the baby King James VI was lowered so that he could eventually present English speakers with the Bible in their own tongue. It is, perhaps, too early yet to assess whether this improved the national character of either England or Scotland.

The Tattoo

That great military ballet, the Tattoo is and was held during the Edinburgh Festival each year, with pipes and drums and bangs and military music. These very popular entertainments are still held on the castle esplanade—i.e., its parade ground. Cleared of all buses and cars for this piece of theatre, a scaffolding was erected there, rising thirty feet above the parade ground. Tiers of planks formed the spartan seating and it was left to the tourist guide to work out just where his customers were to be placed in this darkened latter-day amphitheatre, resembling more a wooden spider web than any military structure.

It was he who had to fetch and pay for cushions to ease the aching behind of people who had not quite appreciated the fact that they were in the hands of the British army, which habitually did things the hard way. At the end of the show, the tour guide was faced with the problem of getting his group safely back to their small hotel in the suburbs. The tidal wave of spectators leaving the Tattoo threatened to overwhelm the city transport, but somehow it never quite did so.

Small Hotels

These small suburban hotels that relied so heavily on the foreign students booked into them [at special rates] were a strange assortment. There was one on Learmonth Terrace, a smart part of the city, run by a Polish owner and his Scottish wife. They ran a good standard of hotel and were slowly consolidating and expanding into adjacent buildings on the terrace. It was rumoured that their barman had been a general in the Polish army, but, to my shame, I thought it was a leg pull and so missed a chance to speak to a bit of WWII history. I might even have learned something. I enjoyed trips that involved a few nights in this comfortable hotel.

At the other end of the scale was an embryo hotel, an establishment formed out of a series of large suburban villas whose gardens had been built over to form a restaurant and kitchens This was run rather amateurishly by a plump, balding man of middle age with a toothbrush moustache. He was somewhat shifty, with strange habits and insisted on flaunting his Jaguar car as a symbol of his prosperity. Perhaps this was an attempt to obscure the fact that the small hotel's accounts constantly hovered between credit and debit. For all his talk of thousands of pounds, he obliged his guests to share a bathroom and toilet between twenty people.

The attentive reader will immediately observe that this was well before en suite WC & Bath were normal offerings even in Bed and Breakfast rooms. The redeeming feature of this 'hotel' was the large servings of good food that its kitchen provided. This place was uncomfortable for the guide, who got a really poky room, resembling an elongated phone booth. The owner was exceptionally generous with Christmas presents for the office at Crichton Street, so the connection was preserved for years.

On the Buses

Thanks to frequent day trips to the Trossachs, that popular beauty spot at the gateway to the Highlands, I became very friendly with one elderly bus driver in particular. Jock Peggie was the first driver that I got to know well. As I mentioned before, it was he who drove the French tourists to 'The Baillie Nicol Jarvie' on my very first expedition out of Edinburgh. He was in his mid-fifties, a smallish man with a face tanned by sitting for weeks in the glass cockpit of his large modern touring bus. Whether his face was browned by constant exposure to sunlight or by constant exposure to cigarette smoke, its expression was one of furrowed sorrow. Those who knew him best attributed his gloomy visage to extreme boredom with the poor quality of tour guides' stories. This was something to be remedied.

J Peggie didn't own the bus; it belonged to a prosperous company in Dalkeith, but long service gave him the first choice of vehicles, so he chose the best. I was flattered to find that he approved of my line of patter, which consisted mainly of giving the official 'information', followed by a somewhat sceptical examination to test the truth of the story.

"It's the story that matters," said old John to young John. "People remember a good story and with it, they remember their tour. A good story is better than a good joke because a lot of folks have no sense of humour."

Probably, Jock was trying to warn me off juvenile student jokes, and there were plenty of them. He regarded himself as my unofficial tutor, sometimes even giving me a list of landmarks and mountains, stopping points and views. Inevitably, these lists were written on the back of a cigarette packet, often my own almost empty pack of twenty 'Senior Service.' There was no point in pretending that, without Jock's prompting, I knew which of several peaks was Ben Vorlich and which Ben Venacher. Entirely due to JP, I got the story of how the trees in the long valley through the Trossachs were planted to represent the disposition of the armies at the Battle of Waterloo. Although all were pines of some description, these massive groups were of distinctly different colours to distinguish between French, British and Prussian. There was even one tiny clump of trees at the end of the display, which was said to represent Napoleon running away.

Loch Lomond

Trips to the Trossachs could sometimes be combined with a sail on Loch Lomond. Tourists and trippers may have known absolutely no Scottish history and may have been completely indifferent to the clans and tartans, but every one of them knew of Loch Lomond and most of them could sing about high roads and low roads. The strange thing about this beautiful stretch of water was that the whereabouts of the steamer boarding place were almost invisible from the road. Surrounded by numerous small piers and jetties, the official steamer boarding place was to be found at the tail of the Loch in Balloch/Alexandria, hidden behind an estate of council houses. Scottish egalitarianism had decreed that the homes of the poor had just as much right as the homes of the rich to despoil a beauty spot.

Jock Peggie introduced me to the simple method of skimming a little off the top of a tourist deal, whereby nobody loses because such a thing is already factored into the ticket price. When we arrived at Balloch landings, Jock would ask everyone to please remain seated while he took directions from the ticket office as to which boat the trip would be using. To use the official 'Maid of the Loch' steamer entailed a six to eight-hour journey, while the bus operators had only calculated a two-hour stop. Logic or logistics, therefore dictated that we use one of the independent motor boats, of which there were plenty.

His system was, as already stated, simple. Jock went to two or three competing owners of motor boats, saying to each, "I have a group ticket for twenty [or thirty] passengers. What do you offer?" [meaning how much per head for giving you this business?]. JP had his regulars but sometimes found that he had to try other boat owners who were not already booked. He generally secured about ten shillings a head and would split the resulting money with me. Not all drivers were so generous, but JP was not just anybody.

A Guide on Foot

The main drawback with guiding bus tours is that the visitor can only be given a superficial introduction to a series of historical facades and unrelated facts. Walking the length of the Royal Mile, looking into every alleyway or close, and scanning the Blue Guide for details of every ancient house, would take too long for the average visitor. It was, however, the only way to build up a good background to account for this one street and to place it in the position of importance to Edinburgh that its history demanded.

At a superficial first glance, this appeared to be an afternoon's job, but even after a winter spent exploring this puzzling, heavily inter-folded street with its cobbles and high tenements, I still had only a passing knowledge of the Royal Mile. This was the way that Edinburgh drew me ever closer in its tweedy mist or Haar.

The shops along this foggy street were a curious mixture of genuine antique dealers, expensive kilt-makers, print dealers, picture framers, second-hand bookshops and the inevitable woollens and tweed shops. One of the antique shops was particularly favoured by the Queen Mother, while another had a special interest in Russian Orthodox icons; almost worthless then, thirty years later, they changed hands at stellar prices. Real treasures were still to be found among low-cost kitsch.

Tartan tat was rather frowned on in those days: it was too obviously catch penny and lowered the tone of the Royal City. Unfortunately, this august mile terminated in a brewery with a stinky gents' toilet right opposite the gates of the Royal Palace of Holyrood House. In a fortunate turn of events, the brewery and its toilet have been replaced at Holyrood by the sober if strange buildings of the Scottish Parliament. Less fortunately, this has, in its turn, given material to jokers who want to poke fun at stinking politics and badly organised parties at a brewery.

The Old Mile of 1958 contained several good quality shops specialising in knitwear, woollens, swatches of cloth and tweed clothing. As I poked around these many and various shops, it struck me forcibly that these goods were priced much, much higher than the same things in the factory shops in the Borders to which we took our visitors. Obviously, there was a considerable markup involved in this line of business and Jock confirmed this. He and I, it seemed could always get a free meal in the factory canteen when we brought in a bus load of tourists to a mill shop. He didn't reveal his capitation fee.

More About Tour Guiding

A simple and quite innocent scheme presented itself to me, a discount-sharing co-operative, in fact. The student tourists, mainly from the USA were informed that a certain high-quality wool, tweed and tartan shop would give them a discount on all purchases above a certain total amount. They were urged to retain all their receipt slips for US Customs and for a scheme that might yield a further discount. I had negotiated beforehand with the shop in question a percentage of sales to my group. Although the shop owner was delighted with the afternoon's sales, fifteen hundred pounds, he nevertheless jibbed at the size of the fee that he owed me. He said, "Next time, we'll make it two per cent, not ten."

A large sum was divided pro rata among the young students, who, although grateful, nevertheless were puzzled that anyone should give away money; that was unAmerican, perhaps even socialist. It was interesting how smartly they responded to the little motto: 'From each according to his means; to each according to his needs.' Was that Marx or Sermon on the Mount? It doesn't matter.

A Spanish Jaunt

As my reward for goodness knows how many trips around the Trossachs and about twenty tours of Edinburgh, I was given a trip to the Balearic Island of Ibiza. This struck me as odd because the Crichton Street office knew that I could speak French and German but of Spanish, I had not even a smidgen. The prospect of a holiday in the Mediterranean sunshine was nevertheless very appealing, so I collected the usual bundle of tickets and timetables, together with a small float of cash for use in emergencies. Just in case of such emergencies, I bought a pocket-size Spanish-English dictionary.

The very knowledgeable elderly lady at Thin's bookshop smiled as she handed me the wrapped book and said, "You do know that there are at least three languages that you might encounter, don't you? General Franco has banned all except the official and classic Spanish, but that doesn't mean that the others are never used."

En Route

This job got off to a bad start. The cheap student accommodation recommended by the National Union of Students turned out to be a B&B in Lewisham. It was run on very pinch penny lines by some balding bachelor whose idea of breakfast was good, but whose version of bed was not. I was squeezed under the kitchen table on a mattress. As a result of the inevitable dispute about full payment for this rotten arrangement, I left half payment in a handful of silver coins on the table and left. SUS at Crichton Street backed me up.

At Waterloo Station, some twenty Scottish students waited under the giant clock. Where else should strangers to London appoint as a meeting point? They were fairly evenly divided between males and females and between them, represented every University in Scotland. We were all going to have a seaside holiday in Ibiza, a place none of us had ever heard mentioned. Don't forget, this was 1958 and Spain was still an international pariah under a fascist dictator, with a legal system that had tolerated state-organised concentration camps with forced labour and mass executions. Spain was on sufferance, tolerated by Western Europe, wooed by the USA for air bases, but nobody's friend.

Its only attraction to holiday makers was cheap sunshine, cheap food and cheap wine. For criminals, its main attraction lay in its outlaw status; as a result, nobody could get at them because Spain's fascist government refused to make extradition treaties. Presumably, this was because it was still harbouring Nazi war criminals as paying guests.

A Long Train Ride

Waterloo Station to Ibiza was four major train journeys and two ferry crossings spread over forty-plus hours, depending on tides and timetable difficulties. I refer to the latter because, in those days, Spanish railways' published timings were not 100% reliable. In all innocence, Esme and Mireille in Crichton Street had timed this long journey with reference to the officially published timetables, leaving an hour or so between arrivals and departures, but events in Barcelona took over and produced a characteristic AMFU. More of this in its proper place.

The boat train from Waterloo to Dover docks was a high-speed spree through the green garden of England. A twin-funnel British Rail ferry was waiting for us as though posing for a travel advertisement: black and yellow funnels against the white cliffs and green sea, the whole scene lit by brilliant sunshine. Everything beckoned the traveller to the prospect of an idyllic channel crossing.

The guide's task was to get twenty suitcases and twenty students safely aboard the ferry and to tip the porters with their large trolley. Efficient dockside porters were important in getting numerous bits of group luggage from the train and up the right gangplank on the right ferry. Of course, a trolley full of bags attracted porters, who could be sure of a decent tip, which was by no means the case with the average foot passenger. The same system worked in Boulogne with the dockside porters booking clients verbally even before the ferry had tied up to the quay. Twenty bags was an attractive task for porters in Dover and Boulogne and they pointedly showed their enamel number badges in an effort to ensure that the guide did not place his business elsewhere.

The French SNCF express shot us into Paris, Gare du Nord and twenty individuals had then to maul their baggage through the tunnels of the Metro to arrive at the Gare de L'Orient where the train to Portbou on the Spanish frontier awaited them. There followed a fourteen-hour journey the length of France.

There was something quite unique about a long night time rail journey, sitting upright against the cold glass of the carriage window as numerous small stations flashed by. All clad in white pyjamas of concrete, their blackened windows emphasised their repose, while, at the same time, they were all seemingly a jingle with the same alarm bells. Major stations came and went without any passengers seeming to alight or to mount the train. There seemed to be no late-night station buffets, even at major junctions. Perhaps the station staff did not want to disturb their clients with hot coffee or stale bread, but Messieurs/Dames Les Voyageurs needed something to ease their aching limbs and stiff necks.

Headache and a dry mouth were common features among those sitting up on the all-night train. Travellers were only too eager to take the guard's advice to get breakfast on the French side of the frontier. For some reason that eluded me, the French railways buffets served breakfast coffee in large bowls, a pint at a time. The croissants, still hot, made up for the almost emetically strong coffee. Then, on into the unknown.

Spain

To the Scottish students, having been prepared by numerous wartime films, the Spanish officials seemed to be imitating actors in a second-rate spy drama. It was sadly the case that some uniform, any uniform seemed to endow the wearer, even the postman with a certain haughtiness, with a scaled-down sense of the Caudillo's power. They were lofty in their tolerance of so many foreigners, but their uniforms were stained and their whole station at Portbou needed a good wash with soap and water. In fact, the reek of blocked drains and stale cabbage spoke of a land of poverty and dirt.

Barcelona, which we reached around two o'clock, confirmed our impression of a breadline economy. The city transport bore on its proud and noble scarlet side the city's coat of arms. Unfortunately, nobody had seen fit to erase from these elderly double-deckers the golden lettering which proclaimed them to be 'LONDON TRANSPORT'. While my student charges were all keen to see the Gaudi cathedral in the city centre, I had some urgent business to attend to with the local National Tourist office. We arranged to meet up at the dockside at 1800hrs in order to board the overnight ferry to Ibiza, San Antonio.

There were ten men and ten women, but tickets for only ten sleeping bunks. As for the return journey, there were no bunks at all. Some mistake, surely?

It was a bit disconcerting to arrive at the tourist agency's smart modern office in the city centre, only to find that it would close at 1500hrs for lunch, returning at 1830hrs. Our ferry was due to sail at 1830hrs. The very pleasant young tourist agent spoke good English. He was sorry about the missing sleeper tickets, but there was extreme pressure at this time of year. He would try to remedy the situation on the return journey and would write to his opposite number in San Antonio. He was confident that something would turn up. Of course, nothing did turn up despite frequent visits to San Antonio and phone calls to Barcelona. We had been short-changed and that's how we would stay.

The nice young travel agent accompanied me to the door, locking it behind us with a flourish. He was going off for lunch and there was nothing more to say. Disappointed and almost powerless, I stood in the centre of a city where most shops were closing for siesta and where most people seemed not to understand my Spanish [for the very good reason that their preferred language was Catalan]. I needed food: French breakfast was, by 1540hrs, a very faint stomach-cramping memory of nine hours ago. It seemed sensible to head for the harbour to locate the ferry and food.

In the optimistic belief that seafarers and taverns tend to flock together, I pointed myself at a gigantic rusty grey structure that stood about 120 feet high and dominated the central harbour. This could have been a piece of modern town sculpture, but it was in fact a three-deck anti-aircraft gun platform, reminding everyone that twenty years previously,

Barcelona had been in the thick of the Spanish civil war. It could possibly have been left there by the Franco government as a symbolic threat to the citizens of Barcelona of the consequences that misbehaviour would incur.

Led by my nose, my hungry belly found food in the form of a generous portion of fish with paella at a dockside tavern. As there was nothing more to be done, I drank the whole carafe of red wine that the waiter plonked unbidden onto the table. The bill, when it arrived, was amazingly little in sterling terms. A small Spanish note covered the meal, the wine and a 15% tip.

At six o'clock, twenty Scottish students turned up at the quayside, but only when their collective ticket was shown were they allowed past the official at the foot of the gangplank. As a precaution, the female students had been warned that they alone could have a sleeping berth. The ship's purser, when tackled on the point, shook his head regretfully and pointed to his full allocation chart. He did, however, mention that 'certain financial arrangements' could possibly secure crews' bunks on our return journey and told me the words to use. As a friendly gesture, he locked all my twenty bags in a secure part of his luggage store.

There was a certain charm about cruising in the warm breeze of a Mediterranean summer evening. The breeze pleasantly refreshed the passengers in the forward part of the ship as they gazed at glowing phosphorescent swirls of light thrown up by the bow wave. It was a calming and beautiful scene, too serene to last. As the first-class dining room emptied onto these same forward decks, the tourist class passengers were ushered to the stern, behind a locked gate.

On the stern decks, the same warm calm evening welcomed the tourists to wrap themselves in a blanket [at 10 pesetas] and settle down for the night crossing. There was a snag. This elderly ferry's diesel engines trailed a thick black vapour trail behind its slow progress through the water. The odour of diesel gradually nauseated more and more sleepers, leading them to seek shelter in the waist of the ship. It was a long and sleepless night for many.

The dawn over the Mediterranean is beautiful, but as drawn out as a Beethoven symphony. Eventually, having established yet another fine summer morning, the sun ushered the ferry into the small, cramped port of San Antonio. Among the dockside workers, there seemed to be a certain unfamiliarity with the various ropes and cables, which delayed the final lowering of the disembarkation gangways. True to form, the student luggage came last, by which time the quayside appeared to be deserted except for four taxis and a man in shirt sleeves standing expectantly on the coils and lines of rope. This was our contact who would take us to our hotel.

Senor Shirtsleeves sorted us into four taxis and we took off, not for somewhere in the town of San Antonio, but for the village of San Antonio Abad fifteen miles to the south. The road surface deteriorated progressively as we approached our destination, finally disappearing into thick sand at the edge of the village. Perhaps the village council had been unable to fund further tarmac. In a cloud of dust, our convoy of taxis ploughed through the main street and halted two hundred metres further on. At an idyllic scene where the track abruptly stopped, cool white-painted stone buildings stood on rough red rocks looking out onto the turquoise sea. Our irritations and doubts fell away from us. This large white hotel with its squat white lighthouse annexe looked perfect.

Our joyful reaction was interrupted by the taxi drivers who, having downloaded our baggage from their rusty iron roof racks, were noisily demanding payment, while a group of students were just as noisily refusing to pay. The trouble had to be explained to Senor Shirtsleeves: taxi number one had made a smart return take-off still with some baggage on the roof rack. Senor S sent one of the other cars off in pursuit. Returning half an hour later, the errant driver found us engaged in yet another dispute. The hotel manager explained that building work on the hotel was still incomplete and that while he could find beds for just eight of us in the lighthouse annexe, the remainder would be farmed out to private homes in the village.

The big white hotel building, with its cool marble veranda shaded by twelve broad arched colonnades, was, alas, no more than a facade with only a dining room and kitchens behind it. Wearily, the students accepted the arrangement and it was a relief later to find that these private B&Bs were very good. There was no hiding the fact that they had been sold short measure yet again.

Bearing in mind that the year was 1958 and that sudden popularity had not yet filled the small villages of Ibiza with tower blocks, each with a sea view and huge hotels, each with its own beach, this was a take-it-or-leave-it situation. There was nowhere else to take my bargain bundle of tourist trade. Any refund that our students were due, and they were certainly owed one, would have to be negotiated in Edinburgh in the months ahead.

Siesta and the GP's Family

There is something about the heat and humidity of noon in Ibiza that quickly made the foreign tourist understand the meaning of and need for a siesta. For this purpose, the great marble veranda, mentioned above, was ideally suited. Equipped with well-padded loungers and a well-stocked bar, it helped me through the long days of heat. A paperback edition of 'Don Quixote' prevented idleness from becoming boredom. The long Spanish siesta is the ideal opportunity to read that long novel that has stood on the bedside table for so many years.

The barman was a jovial young man by the name of Pepe, suitable in view of the fact that his main trade seemed to be in Pepsi Cola with the young children of a Scottish doctor. This good GP and his family were renting a nearby villa, but they made full use of the veranda and bar.

I first came across these children when we were all swimming off a low rocky shelf that doubled up between being a mooring for small boats and a safe entry into the sea for bathers. I found it hard to understand how a Scottish child of four could speak rapid and understandable Spanish [or was it Catalan?] after only six weeks of exposure to the juvenile playgrounds and beaches of San Antonio. The fact remained that it was this four-year-old boy who took his father shopping at the fruit and vegetable stalls that stood around the harbour. It was he also who took me by the hand and led me to meet his father.

This very affable young GP, rounded and sleek, was enjoying a six months holiday away from his regular job with a large oil company in Nigeria. His contract, it seemed, allowed him six months leave every twelve months as he worked as part of a large medical team looking after a base hospital and about 10,000 people. The work pleased him and he felt well rewarded, especially by the big pharmaceutical companies who deeply appreciated the large annual drug contracts that were his to award. His wife was also appreciative of the liberal supply of housemaids and cooks in Nigeria but did not much enjoy the isolation of living in the vast fenced and guarded compound of the oil company. She preferred her own home in Helensburgh and was determined that her children would be privately educated in Scotland.

The fruit market and fish market were regular features that drew me to the harbour. Local fishermen tended to lounge around their boats moored here. The large acetylene lanterns fixed in each stern indicated that most of their fishing was nocturnal. There was no question of striking up a casual conversation with these boatmen, but with the doctor's four-year-old as my interpreter, I negotiated an afternoon boat ride down the coast. Times, numbers, prices and venue were all agreed upon. What could possibly go wrong?

A Sail Round the Bay
Involves Trouble

This was a foolish question to ask in the Spain of 1958. Some twelve young Scots clad in shorts and carrying towels were picked up promptly at 1400hrs from the rocky ledge landing place. The day was perfect; the sea was calm; the sands along the coast line sparkled white and pure. The fishermen hoisted a red sail once we had cleared the rocks and the sleek green, red and white rather Moorish ship, with its sharp high bow, spanked along in front of a warm breeze for about an hour. We came to a small rocky, deserted bay, surrounded by trees and thick green bushes, probably olives. There we swam in the clear turquoise water and ate the packed lunch supplied by the hotel before our departure. Everything seemed wonderful.

We returned to the rocky ledge at about six-thirty and settled up with the boat owners. No sooner had they put the cash in their pocket, than another crowd of fishermen appeared, and it must be admitted that two of them looked familiar. This second lot indignantly accused us of breaking our arrangement and demanded payment for the business that was rightfully theirs. An ugly scene threatened to develop between a dozen brown and weatherbeaten tough fishermen and a couple of pink young Scots. Like a Deus ex machina from an ancient drama, there suddenly appeared Pepe. Speaking in the local dialect, he calmed things down and rather curtly sent the fishermen, boats and all, on their way back to the harbour.

Only then was it revealed that Pepe spoke very good Brooklyn English. The tips, it seemed, were better if he appeared to be making an effort to understand.

"These guys have played this trick on tourists twice this year. I told them the Guarda Civil, would have to decide the matter if they couldn't do it between them."

These armed police might have looked a bit comic opera in their funny black hats, but there was nothing amusing about their behaviour. They were not people to welcome the queries of a lost tourist nor to settle the petty problems of fishermen who felt cheated out of a fee. Ordinary people did not argue with them.

Nightlife

Our tourists' enduring fascination with the night life of San Antonio was fed mainly by a large place whose neon lights declared it to be a 'Boite de Nuit'. It was notable that, as in Britain, impropriety seemed to be excusable if it could be blamed on the French. Entry to the Boite was cheap, drink was freely available and the music was loud and hot. Fundador, a cheap local brandy, was served in a vast variety of cocktails and would make the average Scottish student very drunk within the evening. They loved the atmosphere, they loved each other and they loved their holiday in Ibiza. Above all, they loved the adjustment of their daily clock which allowed them to sleep until midday, swim and sun until lunch at 3 pm, to doze in the shade until 6 pm, followed by more swimming and sunning before drinks with Pepe on the broad veranda. Dinner was at nine-thirty in the evening, after which, the roundabout of carousal started again.

The Spanish word 'siesta' gained widespread use among the sunburned students, while their guide quickly found appropriate words for 'more food' to satisfy their robust appetites. Other words were required for sunburn lotion, which the village pharmacy made up from ground almonds in the same almond oil that fuelled the island buses.

The ramshackle old Italian bus that ran daily to San Antonio reminded me strongly of the old 1934 Albion that patrolled the outlying villages around North Staffordshire during WWII. It had the same rattling windows, the same slatted wooden benches, the same rusty patches front and rear. The main difference was that the fares on the Ibiza bus went up by 10% every few days, but perhaps this was a special tourist 'concession'.

Spanish Efficiency Triggers a Row of Dominoes

After three long bus trips between San Antonio and San Antonio Abad, it became clear that the tourist agency would not or could not supply sleeping accommodation for the Scottish party on its return trip to Barcelona. At the quayside, the ship's purser undertook to find bunks for each of the ten women by buying cabin space from the crew. It cost a lot of paper, but at least the women were spared another queasy, sleepless night on the cold hard planks of the deck.

The ferry's entry into the harbour at Barcelona was delayed by nearly an hour to await the tide. [That, at least, was the excuse, though the Mediterranean has a very small tidal rise and fall.] This cut deeply into the transfer time calculated by the Spanish tourist agency for our party to get to the main railway station before our express to Portbou on the frontier. We didn't make it.

It was at this point that old Spanish customs began to reveal a side of their society that we had not seen, but may have suspected. Having missed our connecting train, our party needed to book reservations on the next train to the frontier. Before this could even be considered, however, permission to travel on this train had to be granted by the station master. His was the office with the big frosted windows and a notice displaying business times: 6 am to 11 am; 1700 pm to 2200 pm. The time was then 1030 and there was a queue of three.

A fat young man in an army uniform who bore the insignia of a major dealt with our request but only after making a lengthy phone call, probably to check on our bona fide status as travelling holiday makers. In reply to our query regarding seat reservations, Fatty said that this was out of the question until tomorrow [at least that is what 'manana' implied]. To him, it was a matter of complete indifference whether we caught a train or slept on the platform. If necessary, he would continue the discussion at 1700hrs.

A Rough Ride Home

The last two coaches on the train had no reserved seats, so obviously, these were our only hope if we wanted to travel. We very much did want to travel by the very next train, because it looked as though a whole row of dominoes was about to fall as we missed one connection after another.

Summoning a war council of students, they were given to understand our precarious position. Our train to the frontier would leave at 1200, but would be at the platform "…Oh, hell! It's there now."

With twenty minutes to go, the last two carriages already seemed full. Spaniards were pushing suitcases through the open windows and even the corridors seemed to be filling up, with bags blocking the end doorways. We had twenty bags to squeeze in and we did it by sending two men in over the top of these cases at the doorways to start easing luggage back down the corridor. With merciless pushing, we forced the Scottish bags onto the train and were able to close the door just as the guard blew his whistle for departure.

The journey to the frontier was sweaty and cramped in the small confined space outside the end toilet. We were lucky, in a way, that this toilet stank so abominably that nobody cared to use it. Portbou and the change of trains at the frontier was literally a breath of fresh air, though the drains there still needed unblocking.

To enter the French express, routed directly to Boulogne, was to return to normality. The French guard passed our group ticket with a nonchalant wave and invited us to take our choice of seats as this train was only very lightly booked for the first 100km.

We were able to stretch out and catch up on some of our lost sleep. The rest of the journey was uneventful and left no marks on my memory. As for Spain and the Spanish, I was able to revise my opinions some forty years later, when I found a completely different country and a much more agreeable people.

Back to Crichton Street

A trickle of Ibiza sand fell from my leather neck pouch as I shook from it a selection of Spanish pesetas, receipts, used vouchers and train tickets. Esme Walker, the boss woman and chief of SUS Travel looked at the mess on her desk and then at the chaos in my report. After a series of disasters, irritations, disappointments and near misses, it seemed inevitable that my performance would be viewed as less than a success. It was a surprise, therefore, to receive warm praise from Esme. The Ibiza business deal would be renegotiated with our Spanish counterparts, with a view to withholding some money, she said, so that the students could be reimbursed some money.

While the iron was still hot in the tourist office smithy, Esme struck, "You'll need to go to Glasgow tomorrow to meet forty US students arriving on the 'Empress of India' at Greenoch at three in the afternoon. Accommodation is fixed with the Glasgow University Halls of Residence and meals are arranged there. If you feel strong enough, you can take a few down the Byres Road for a drink: it's one damned pub after another for half a mile. Jock Peggie will pick you up here at noon and take the whole lot for a three-day tour of the Highlands. There's a nice easy job for you! Don't forget to sign your expenses schedule for Ibiza."

A Trip Down Byres Road

The forty miles or so to Glasgow from Edinburgh had to be ground out on the old A8, a road with a fearful reputation for delays and accidents. J Peggie and I got into Greenock around 2.30 pm and slowly nudged our bus to the quayside. It was raining and the 'Empress' stood about half a mile offshore like a white cloud in a silver mist.

Passengers were offloaded onto a floating platform in the deep water, from which a large ferry boat further transported them ashore in the shallows.

There was a pipe band there to greet them in style as they set foot in Scotland, but the rain started to turn their music to a gurgle. They moved into the reception hall and struck up again as the Empress picked up her skirts and departed for Liverpool with the remaining 850 passengers. The misty rain followed us into Glasgow and wetly ushered the tourists into the stone university buildings where they were to spend the night.

It was good solid accommodation and most of the student tourists seemed to opt for a hot shower before supper. After this, some dozen or so young ladies gathered around me and requested to be shown 'the sights'. As this was to be the feature of the morning, they were persuaded to settle for a look at Byres Road, Glasgow's answer to Montmartre. Jock Peggie didn't fancy a set of adolescents as drinking partners, but he wrote the name of two pubs which were to be avoided at any time and on any occasion. They were football pubs and didn't welcome outsiders.

A few yards down Byres Road and with a dozen young women in tow, a very large and smart-looking pub appeared to be welcoming us. Two burly men in white shirt sleeves each wearing a large white apron stood outside the door.

"You're no coming in," they greeted us. "The Polis is inside. There's been trouble."

The rain was starting again and it became a matter of urgency to find a friendly bar.

This should have been a mere walk across the road, but this was Glasgow in 1958. Another large set of double doors beckoned us to enter, every last thirteen of us.

"OUT. You're no coming in with they women!"

Yet another nearby bar, but this time, I went in first and left the women huddled in the doorway. Then I asked the question that should have been put in the first place, "Have you got a ladies' room?"

Receiving an affirmative, my rather damp young women came inside to fill a rather poky glass window-lined cubicle and to sample true Glasgow pub bonhomie. In those days, women sat at the bar or in the saloon bar in only the lowest pubs and this one was very respectable. It preserved its male customers from the unwanted attentions of disreputable women while doing nothing to discourage them from leering at perfectly innocent girls through the glazing of the ladies' room. Luckily, these youngsters just regarded it all as 'local colour'.

Touring buses present any city as just a series of moving pictures, devoid of any sound other than that of the guide's voice. There was a lot to be seen in old Glasgow, but, as with Edinburgh, it was best seen on foot. We managed to park the bus centrally so that our tourists could enter St Mungo's Cathedral to view Dali's Christ on the Cross, entitled 'The Saviour of the World'. We swooped from the cathedral to Provand's Land nearby, the last surviving piece of medieval Glasgow, and then took off for Loch Lomond.

Off to Kingussie

We put the students on the official steamer at Balloch and then headed the bus north to meet them again some 20 miles up the Loch. That put us 20 miles ahead on our road to Kingussie, where a charming white stone-built hotel awaited our arrival. It was Saturday night, the one night of the week when there was much activity in this small Highland village.

On Saturday night, Kingussie became the big city where local boys met local girls and high expectations often flared into love and marriage. The keen focus of 'romance' was the Saturday night hop at the local community centre. In those days, this function was served by a wooden army hut left over from 1918, but its looks were irrelevant to the 100 young people who crowded in.

By nine o'clock, when I appeared at the dance with half a dozen American girls, the tickets were sold out and the wooden hut was full to overflowing. An eightsome reel was in progress, urged on by a fiddler and two accordionists. The sound of whooping was muffled by the stamping of many feet on the wooden floorboards. They were really throwing themselves and their dance partners into top gear. The wooden hut shifted and groaned on its brick supports as more and more horse power was applied. Instead of going on to a more sedate dance, the fiddler started yet another reel and the testing of the old hut continued until eleven o'clock when suddenly everything went silent. The Sabbath was only an hour away.

I looked into the bar of the hotel, knowing just where to find our driver. Jock bought me a drink, two drinks, in fact, because he wanted me to taste Doch and Doruis—whisky with a chaser of beer. So I bought him the same and he bought me another, and so on.

We were due to depart from Kingussie at 0830hrs, which meant an early breakfast and this promised difficulty rousing sleepy young people, so I had promised the US woman leading this tour that I would knock on her door at six-thirty. Unfortunately, I used a North of England expression: 'I'll knock you up at six-thirty'. This, apparently, had an unfortunate meaning in US parlance, but, luckily, it was taken as hilarious, rather than as a threat of sexual violence.

St Andrews

It took a long time to drive from Kingussie to St Andrews in 1958 because the road, the fearsome A9, was [and is still] difficult and dangerous. Despite a small hangover, I found the journey strangely moving, the tall blue mountains flanking steeply banked ranks of hills which would suddenly open out to reveal a shallow silver river rushing its way through the farmland of a broad emerald valley. There was a feeling of energy awaiting its release; of a familiar completeness that seemed to bid me welcome. It was as though my mother was calling me to join the family at the table for supper.

We went by Pitlochry where we inspected the new salmon ladder. Unfortunately, news of this device, built entirely for their convenience, had not reached the salmon. There were no leaping fish, but this did not spoil this wonderful drive through the multicoloured heart of the Highlands.

There was no road bridge over the river Tay in 1958, so Jock had to drive us to Perth and from there along the north coast of Fife to St Andrews. It was a long drive, but we arrived at Russack's Hotel, the property of St Andrews University, in time for an evening meal. This hotel was rather grand for undergraduates of the time, but the US students loved it. After supper, there was impromptu dancing to a three-piece palm court orchestra.

Esme had sent another Edinburgh student guide who knew St Andrews well, to help out with displaying this delightful medieval city to our visitors. Together, we split the duties that evening: he guarded the dancing, while I took the American tour leader and eight others to a performance at the local Byre Theatre. This tiny play house could contain no more than forty people. It was so small and so intimate that when the leading man kissed his leading lady with a smacker, the seats in the front row were wetted with spray. The play was instantly forgettable.

I knew absolutely nothing of the medieval history of St Andrews and the terrible bloodletting of the Reformation. My new colleague, on the other hand, was well-read in the Protestant martyrs and the history of John Knox, who had emerged from imprisonment in the French galleys to become a mighty leader of Scottish religious opinion. The quaint cobbled streets of the Old Town fed into the ruined cathedral and led the earnest tourist to the ruins of the castle. It was my first experience of the Bottle Dungeon, but in later years, my small sons delighted to shuffle and crawl along the tunnel of the counter mine that was dug in the time of Knox when the French besieged the castle.

The Bottle Dungeon is so called because it is shaped like an old wine bottle standing upright with only one entrance/exit. The prisoner was lowered on a long rope down the neck of the bottle and might one day be hauled out by the same means. This awful instrument of doom still evokes shudders of terror at the thought of being left to die in endless darkness, with sea water constantly washing through cracks in the rocks at the whim of the tide. Those Reformation religious people had little time for pity or compromise, which is so often the case with two opposing extremes, each believing absolutely in its own righteousness.

Jock had parked his big bus in the railway station car park, only a hundred yards or so from the clubhouse of the Royal and Ancient. St Andrews in 1958 had a handsome and well-served railway station and the decision to close down this branch line was an illustration of Whitehall's crass ignorance of Scotland and indifference to its tourist trade.

Dean Village

We motored sedately back to Edinburgh along the small roads of Fife to North Queensferry. There the bus boarded a transporter ferry across the Forth, skirting the massive steel girders of the Forth Railway Bridge. This short crossing was crowded in the summer holiday months and generally involved a delay of an hour or so. For all that, it was an exciting incident in a long journey and the tourist could count on seeing at least one train crossing high overhead on the great bridge. Seals delighted to accompany these ferries, playing ahead like a porpoise.

We drove demurely through the shady leafy tunnel of great elms that lined the road to Edinburgh and deposited our passengers at the Learmonth Hotel. It was early evening. In the hour or so before dinner, there was an opportunity to explore the other side of Queensferry Road, with its large houses and mansions. It was a suburb populated by the very well-off, ship owners and law lords. It looked down the steep fall of an ornamental pleasure garden right into the valley of the Water of Leith. There was a way down to the water, indeed this had once been the only road from Queensferry to the city, a way that dropped down to a small stone bridge, while gracefully obscuring a corkscrew twist in a backdrop of tall, branching trees.

A slow walk through the Dean Village, a place whose very existence was still unknown to me revealed a mixture of medieval and Victorian buildings huddled under the Dean Bridge, forming a village in itself. There was a primary school, built by the Board of Guardians for Education, built about 1885 and three small shops, one of which doubled as a branch post office. There was a large stone warehouse where a defunct wheel was revealed to have formerly been a watermill. This, presumably was the old mill by the stream, Nellie Dean.

The Water of Leith, a small river seemed at one time to have powered several mills along its length: e.g., Cannon Mill, Silver Mill, Powder Mill. In 1958, the Water of Leith supplied water to the soaking pits of Leggats' skin factory, right next to a handsome red sandstone courtyard tenement building. This was the Well Court, so named because, when it was built in 1884 there was a drinking water pump to supply the needs of the occupants of the 50 or so small apartments. This courtyard of flats was built for the workpeople of the *Scotsman* newspaper by its owner. In the interest of improving the condition of his employees, the buildings incorporated a large hall for social activities, a large clock tower to ensure good timekeeping and a caretaker to ensure behaviour in obedience to a book of rules.

Well-to-do people, living high up in the big houses around Randolph Cliff and Drumsheugh Gardens—i.e., in the expensive part of central Edinburgh—might have regarded Dean Village as a slum, but it strongly appealed to me. One day, I thought, my home will be in Dean Village, in the Well Court. And so it would eventually be.

Touring in 1959

1959 was an election year when the absence of events seemed to indicate that things were getting back to normal after the upsets of Suez in 1956. Eastern European countries and half the Adriatic were closed to tourism by various communist dictators. Greece was virtually unapproachable by land as few people felt strongly enough about Greek antiquities to brave 40 hours or more on a sealed train rolling slowly by obscure routes through a spy-obsessed communist Yugoslavia. Esme was not the least worried: sea, sand and sunshine continued to dominate the very simple tastes of the students of the Fifties.

Having done six weeks of the Trossachs, The Highlands, Edinburgh Castle, the Old Town, the New Town and the Tattoo, there came my way what everybody in the SUS Travel Bureau regarded as a prize job: fourteen days in Paris.

Paris in August

There's always some flaw in the perfect picture: Paris in August was a city without citizens; a city given over to tourists. My tourists all spoke French and seemed to be postgraduate language students pursuing some PhD project or pursuing a sweetheart. We were all easily accommodated in a vast university students' hall just behind the Bou Mich, as those in the know liked to refer to the Boulevard St Michel at the heart of the university area. There, with 200 bedrooms and a full-time residential staff, the Sorbonne treated its resident students like guests in a three-star hotel. With the aid of our newly issued Sorbonne ID cards, we could get breakfast, lunch and supper in any of the university's many dining rooms dotted around Paris, but mainly in the Cite Universitaire, miles out in the suburbs at the end of an exclusive Metro line.

As all the Scottish students had everything about their stay planned and as none of them had any interest in doing official tours or indeed, of doing anything in a group, their guide found himself wandering around the hot and dusty parkland around the Champs Elysee and visiting one art gallery after another. This was my third visit to Paris and my most boring one.

I had first seen it as a schoolboy in 1950 and thought it absolutely dazzling. My second visit had been in 1957, just before embarking on my medical studies, and had confirmed my initial impression of delight. In company with an old schoolmate, I had climbed the Eiffel Tower [mainly by elevator], seen the museum at the Louvre and been engulfed in Notre Dame. The lone guide took himself off to the Palace of Versailles and had a long wander around the vast campus of the University City.

By chance, I struck up a friendship with the senior guardian of the student residence and found myself invited along to witness one of the rare graduation ceremonies at the Ecole Superieur. This, did I but know it, was regarded as France's most illustrious academic degree; from its graduates were [and probably still are] chosen the members of the senior civil service. The ceremony took place in an imposing building faced with tall columns and high stone arches which had all the dusky dignity of a cathedral. There were, nevertheless, no prayers and no hymns. The French took secular pride in avoiding such things on a public occasion, and the ceremony was not the less impressive for that omission.

In appreciation of this experience, it seemed suitable to organise a small drinks party in my room and to summon the Scottish students to give thanks to their French hosts.

Drinks parties always attract unexpected guests, and this was no exception. The concrete corridors of the residence drummed with the rhythms of a transistor radio that just materialised out of nowhere. People in dressing gowns came to complain about the noise and found themselves holding a glass of wine and enjoying a conversation. It must be confessed, certainly, that some surprise was expressed at the fact that the host had used a bidet as a wine cooler. My friend from the management joked on the subject that the British think a bidet is for washing babies in, whereas the French think it is for washing babies out!

I managed to get a ticket for La Boheme at the Opera, but it was a performance strictly for tourists by a provincial company grabbing its moment of glory in out-of-season August. I cannot remember the name of the company, but their performance was delightful and certainly pleased their audience.

Finally, out of sheer boredom, I went to the cinema to see a French documentary which explained how the Resistance and the French Army had single-handedly liberated France in World War Two. I felt sure President De Gaul had approved its contents, for the French, like the British had great difficulty in letting go of past glory.

1960, The Final Tour

The Scottish Union of Students expected me to be fully conversant with all aspects of touring by 1960, but, of course, I wasn't. Having, with the help of another student guide, successfully squired eighty female students from the US Duke University round Kingussie and St Andrews, it seemed a double-barrelled compliment to escort them to Tyne Commission Quay at Newcastle and to see them safely aboard the weekly ferry to Oslo. Having done that, I was to pick up a group of bus tourists at Keswick. They again were US University students, who, having done England—i.e., London and Oxford—were northward bound for Scotland. No problem!

Incompetence in Pullman Luxury

The midday train to Newcastle was a special Pullman train, an upmarket version of ordinary first class. It was a luxury restaurant floating on the rails behind an express steam engine. Passengers sat at lamplit tables for four with curtains at the windows. The elegant carriage seated eighty. It was a poor man's version of the Orient Express with shiny brasses and smart cream, brown and gold paintwork. Alas, such wonders were right outside my limited experience.

At the last minute, by holding my roadmap upside down, I thought there was an obvious problem: there was no provision for feeding these people. By presuming that I was the only one who could see the full picture, I created my greatest grand international cock up [GICU]. The mere memory is enough to give me indigestion.

There was on Waverley Station a British Rail Catering office. Rushing in there, I explained my problem: that I had a party of eighty who were booked onto the train which would depart in ninety minutes. Eighty packed lunches were ordered and paid for out of expenses and eighty large white lunch boxes were duly loaded onto the Pullman train with five minutes to spare.

The smart white-jacketed staff of the Pullman coach were upset. They were preparing a cooked lunch for their eighty passengers and now it looked like being cancelled at the last minute. I had no idea that the Pullman ticket included a cooked lunch: we didn't have such luxuries in Stoke on Trent where I grew up. Some diplomacy had to be applied to the white-coated attendants, and some folding money had to change hands to replace the tips that would not appear as a consequence of my stupidity. Further diplomacy would have to be deployed for Crichton Street.

We changed trains at Newcastle for the short hop down to Tyne Commission Quay and I expected at any minute to receive recriminations from my party of very vocal young people. Instead of anger, I was overwhelmed by their gratitude and found myself robbed of my Tyrolean hat. It was returned to me as the Duke students boarded the night ferry to Oslo. My hat then contained nearly a hundred pounds. Was the tour as good as that?

Overnight in Keswick
More Incompetence

By this time, my career as a tour guide was flowing swiftly down the loo. I was expected back in Crichton Street that afternoon, but somehow it had lodged in my addled mind that I was immediately to go to Keswick and did so exactly and with despatch. So the black stain of incompetence widened and deepened.

Travel east to west by train or indeed, by road was poor in 1960, so it took six hours to cover the sixty miles from Newcastle to Keswick. Then I had to find some sort of Bed and Breakfast place. In the morning, precious coins were spent ringing Esme in Edinburgh to report progress, only to find that the rendezvous was wrong: the next lot of students would be arriving the following morning at 11.30. There then followed a rather acidic, gale-force legalistic expose of my position, which could be best summarised as:

a) You owe SUS Tours forty pounds for the unauthorised purchase of eighty box lunches.

b) You got yourself into this mess by not listening to your verbal briefing, so you can get yourself out of this mess.

c) Your trip to take a tour of the Olympic games in Rome is being reconsidered, as you have become rather unreliable.

Thank goodness that I had made no mention of my hatful of pound notes. That minimised some of the mess.

The Lake District can be a rather dreary place in rainy weather and I had no coat with me; after all, I had expected to spend my time in a bus or train, not walking aimlessly through the watery streets of Keswick. There was not even a cinema in this village or small town. It was a very boring afternoon that had to be blown away by a three-course meal at one of the better hotels. It cost nearly a pound. These extravagant places were easy to find, simply by counting the number of private cars parked outside.

Rose Street

The US students duly arrived and swapped tour guides. They were a party of forty, again from Duke. They were in the charge of an older young woman who was or had been married to a member of the USAF stationed just outside Oxford. Her ignorance of the world, of Britain in particular, was matched by her almost completely blank mind on everything outside art history. The shades of difference between various political opinions did not interest her. The NHS, the welfare state and the British Rail were all equally communist shackles on freedom of choice. She was just another example of a mind trained to answer a limited range of academic questions but otherwise empty. It seemed very possible that her husband had abandoned their marriage as being a non-stop fight with Br'er Rabbit's tar baby.

The other young women displayed the usual delightfully fresh minds of youth. Bearing in mind my experience in a Glasgow pub when I tried to enter with a group of women, I cautiously enquired about the situation in Ma Scott's Bar on Rose Street, a street of 15 bars. The barman thought me a shade of barmy. "Of course, you can bring 'em in. This isn't Byres Road." He was right, of course. Even in those days of long ago, Edinburgh pubs could be very jolly places, with song and music breaking out all over.

We had an entertaining evening in various Rose Street bars and found ourselves joined by various amiable young men who seemed to be very acceptable to the ladies of Duke. As so often happened with Edinburgh youth, they knew of various parties going on in the locality and my large group of young women slowly dissolved like a sugar cube, first into fragments and finally into two or three individuals whom I escorted back to the Learmonth Hotel. Their elderly big sister escort had already gone to bed.

A Long Train Journey to Rome

Esme in Crichton Street had been let down by two would-be student guides who were having problems with the degree examiners in their various specialities. There were two parties going to the Olympic games in Rome, but other tours to Italy and Spain lacked a guide. I had had enough of Spain in 1958, but felt well-disposed to Italy, the scene of my winter tour in 1958. My unnecessary purchase of lunch boxes for the Pullman was excused for the sake of rescuing the tour to Rome, Sorrento and Capri. This time, the stars were in full alignment; the omens were all good. Absolutely nothing would go wrong.

Another long train journey beckoned and had it not been for the presence of a name on the list of travellers on this tour, I, too, might have pulled out. The name was that of a young English woman. We had been acquainted since her school days. More of this later on.

Our train tickets took us from Calais to Rome by way of the Swiss frontier. The bit in between was not specified. We soon found that our train, full of cut-rate tourists, had been diverted away from the busy full-fare routes onto the less used slower alternative link lines. We started from Calais at 3 pm and at 6 pm, found ourselves looking at The Atomium in

Brussels: so we had spent three hours travelling north, instead of south. The train slowly stitched its way through Belgium, then into Luxembourg, and re-entered France at Strasbourg, having paid courtesy calls at various large stations. Passport checks as decreed by the various authorities punctuated this bumbling route. There were small mobile refreshment trollies at the longer halts and they were very welcome because there was no dining car nor drinks bar on this most spartan of trains. Perhaps the assumption was that all passengers on this train for Rome would be athletes on strict diets.

There was nothing at all to differentiate Luxembourg at night from Loughborough. One continuous black vista of countryside reflected the traveller's tired face. Only the large lettering of a name board lent precision to the weary enquiry for the train's whereabouts. Sleep in the upright position on a night journey was generally rewarded with a painful ache in the neck, but whatever it was, whether sleep or boredom, something blotted out our passage through Switzerland. We awoke to the beautiful sight of the sun rising over Lake Garda, its flames of orange and yellow chasing away the night in its purple night gown. We thought that we must be just a couple of hours from Rome.

Rome, Sorrento and Capri

First stop ROME.

Our train slowly and carefully picked its way the length of Italy, which was much bigger than our school atlases would have us believe. At 6 pm, as our train pulled slowly and carefully through the intricacies of line projecting in and out of Rome Central Station, we found ourselves being greeted by a marching street band. Whatever the occasion was for their joyful celebration, it roused our weary travellers to fresh levels of cheerful anticipation. A good omen, I thought.

Mindful of my first visit to Rome Central, I got my tourists in a group and set off to book official taxis. These were the only taxis allowed to enter the station: the cowboy cabs had to stand outside. Four taxis came and without bother we set off for our hotel. The evening was darkening the sky as we left the elegant station buildings, revealing the huge neon letters: PAN AMERICAN AIRWAYS. The first time that I saw it in 1958, it seemed to me to be tempting fate to write boldly underneath: '150 million miles without an accident' and to keep the score running continually. It took forty years, but, inevitably, fate rubbed out the proud total.

Our comfortable hotel at the edge of the central part of Rome seated its student guests at a long table in an airy dining room. Attentive waiters heaped spaghetti in volcanic heaps, exclaiming 'Vesuvio' as they poured the accompanying sauce into the volcano's centre. It was a sight to behold these starving young people set about this meal. Some had obvious experience with stringy pasta, but many young ladies pecked away nervously with knife and fork at a dish that requires twisting between a fork and spoon. Many years later, their British granddaughters would be handling spaghetti and even chopsticks as though they were to the manner born.

Summer 1960 in Rome was very hot and the resultant sunburns hit the young women of the tour around their exposed shoulders, forcing them to buy silk scarves for protection. Luckily, the Roman shops had a wide and wonderfully varied choice of good silk scarves and dresses. The unusually hot sun also introduced to them the idea of a short siesta in the afternoon The Fountains of Trevi tempted sun-scorched people to trail their arms in its cool waters. A special official guardian warned off any boorish youngsters from bathing in the fountains. In no time at all, a popular film ['Three Coins in the Fountain'] would make this guardian's job impossible.

An official guide was hired to take us through the antique ruins of the old city and this led us to the subterranean catacombs, dark, scary, but beautifully cool. We learned the meaning of the phrase 'grotesque', but understanding did not induce any liking for these ugly little carvings. Our souls may have been elevated by thoughts of the early Christians hiding from a cruel death in these caves, but our bodies cried out for cold drinks.

Cool night brought welcome relief and with it the opportunity to visit the open-air opera at the 'Thermi Di

Caracala' where we heard a memorably beautiful performance of Cavalleria Rusticana and I Pagliacci, those two pieces most favoured for death and destruction by the untutored voices of our Amateur Operatic societies.

Second Stop, Sorrento

Our hotel in this large village made famous in song, was modestly called 'The Orangery' and was perched on a cliff top looking out to sea, about one mile from the village square. The bushy trees that flanked and guarded it from the busy access road to Sorrento were indeed laden with oranges. Orange trees shaded the 'al fresco' dining area, where wonderful local dishes, cooked by the proprietor, were served to his guests by his daughters. It was almost idyllic. 'Almost' has to be inserted as a precaution, because there were drawbacks.

Sorrento was in itself an overrated seaside village. The beach was tiny and difficult to access. There was little sand or room for swimming in its tight steep, rocky bay. Far too much room was taken up by old-fashioned horse-drawn bathing 'machines' and they had to be hired. That was all very well, but sharing a wheeled bathing hut between men and women demands quite a lot of patience and tact. There was a bus service to the centre, but so occasional that we found ourselves walking down the twisting descent on a road made of hewn masonry, blackened by long use in its long life. This sturdy old road, nevertheless served to emphasise a feeling of stability and permanence about Sorrento that contrasted strongly with the behaviour of the more youthful locals. The waiters and barmen, mostly in their twenties, were too often smart Alecs who short-changed tourists and tried to pick up the girl students. These local young men obviously regarded my young women as tempting targets and when some of them accepted an offer of a lift back to our clifftop hotel from a couple of smoothies, I jumped into the car first and upset their calculations. The lift was given with a rather poor grace and attempts at further dating. Hard luck!

A bus tour took us to Amalfi, where the sea was warm and green and the whole rocky hillside village sparkled and delighted the eye. Amalfi was one of the few tourist jewels that familiarity had neither cheapened nor tarnished. We swam in the turquoise sea and gazed longingly at the beautiful tapestry of green trees and white houses.

Another bus tour took us to the ruins of Pompeii, where the Italian guide to the site coyly suggested that some of the domestic murals may offend the ladies. Of course, these were the very pictures that they insisted on viewing. The ruins of Pompeii, with their reminder of the transience of human life rather dampened the chatter in the bus as we returned to The Orangery, but it may equally well have been the weariness induced by walking in the hot sun all afternoon.

Last came Capri. This beautiful island is best described as a verdant rock set in a sea of jade: it was an experience quite apart from the ordinary. It was too small to support the vast inflow of tourists and had to be supplied with drinking water by a small coastal tanker that called every day. There were no roads and no motor vehicles. Footpaths took the visitor up the steep winding hill from the port to the main town. Small pathways wiggled their way all across this tiny overpopulated island, making all visitors exercise as they explored.

Where else but in Capri could a group of young people stop in the narrow twisting street to listen to the music of a violin played high above on a second-floor balcony and find themselves summoned by the player to come upstairs for a drink?

A Pan-like little man in his early sixties greeted us with fiddle and bow in hand. For half an hour, he played while we danced on the polished parquet of a large sitting room. Then it was all over. Our Italian was inadequate to thank him properly, we did not even know his name, but we shook his hand warmly and said 'Areviderci'. That evening, there was a public music concert in an open-air amphitheatre. It had a lot in common with the anatomy lecture theatre back home at Edinburgh Medical School, including very hard seats. I looked for Pan in the gloom of the orchestra area, but the dim lights on the music stand illuminated very little.

At this point in the story, there reappeared the young woman acquaintance of my youth with whom this account of a student tour to Italy opened. She was the dazzling girl who had danced with me to Pan's music that afternoon. Under a starlit black velvet Mediterranean sky; to a background of soft music, we agreed that eventually there may be a future for us together.

The return journey from Capri to Naples was by way of the passenger 'aliscafi', a fast motor boat that skimmed over the waves on catamaran skis. Thereby lay a problem, because waves, even on a calm day, form a series of ridges similar to a ploughed field. The Neapolitan boatman needed to keep to his scheduled timetable and possibly also wanted to show off the speed of his vessel. This rattling, bumpy ride was exciting for some and nauseating for others, so a rather subdued group mounted the long-distance express for Rome and Paris.

The Germans have nice descriptive names for their different types of trains: 'bummelzug' is the slow pottering provincial train, whereas, the fast direct train is the 'D-zug'. There was a vast difference in comfort and speed between the cheap fare holiday train that had slowly ground its way across half of Western Europe and this express carrying us back to Rome and Paris.

Twenty-four hours after leaving Naples, we parted company in London. It had been a most memorable holiday for all of us and reluctant farewells marked possible budding affairs. Holiday romances were always rather fragile things but one at least held good for sixty-five years.

Loch Lomond No More

This final tour to Italy was a resounding success and the good news poured into Crichton Street like a flood from an overflowing bath tub. Rome, Sorrento and Capri starred for many years through the sixties and after. Reluctantly, I handed in my Sherif's badge and six-shooters to Esme. Clinical years lay ahead of me and they made heavy demands on medical students' vacation time. There was also the question of allocating time to the beautiful young criminologist who had danced with me on the Isle of Capri.

We married the following year but fate and the demon of Scottish Students' Travel Service had not yet finished with me.

Preparations for a Bride

Somewhere else I have written about how, as a slightly older student, I had sold my rather flashy sports car before entering medicine at the age of 24. This money, five hundred and fifty pounds, enabled me to buy outright a small flat in the Dean Village. It was sparingly furnished with cast-off items from my parents' home and with the help of the auction rooms on George Street, either Dowells or Lyon and Turnbull. The finished effect pleased me greatly, but I quickly realised that the presence of a wife would demand certain additional features, such as a wardrobe large enough to accommodate the clothes of two people. The bedrooms were small.

A double bed left a gap a mere two and a half feet between the bed and wall down the long side and the same again at the window. The auctioneer took pity on me at last and pointed out that a small wardrobe, such as I required did not exist and would have to be made by a cabinet maker. As the standard width of a wardrobe was five feet, he jokingly suggested that it might be best to buy a full-size second-hand cupboard at his auction and cut it down the middle to form two halves thirty inches by thirty inches.

As a matter of fact, he added, this Victorian walnut wardrobe had failed to sell twice and was available for eight pounds, well, a fiver, seeing as it would cost another four pounds to have it delivered by carrier [of whom there were always several available at the end of an auction].

It was a beautiful piece of wood and it took me some effort to cut and mount the two halves so that the cut edges did not show. Certainly, it squeezed the double bed hard against the wall, but there was just enough shuffle room to change the sheets.

The bedroom sorted, there remained the question of forming a bathroom. I had bought a flat with a WC and a cold water tap at the kitchen sink. Hot water was slowly available from a gas-fired 'Ascot' heater fixed by the kitchen window. The wretched thing had to be lit with a match and always, always exploded with a loud BANG! The kitchen window gave a view of a landing on the common stair and so these explosions occasionally caused neighbours to comment.

The Ascot was not the only kitchen problem. In 1960 Edinburgh, the only hot takeaway food was fish and chips, good for the occasional treat, but not the practical answer to the sort of healthy diet that an aspiring doctor should eat. In short, the kitchen lacked a cooker. The previous owner had taken her gas stove away with her other belongings.

This omission was easily remedied by a quick visit to the rather splendid showrooms on George Street Scottish Gas. So large was this showroom and so well supplied with polite and attentive staff that this rather shabby student, having stated the problem, was immediately taken to the 'reconditioned appliances'. The charming lady of mature years who waltzed me around various gas stoves checked my note of the space available and said, "You really ought to get a fridge as well and I have a gas fridge here that will just fit. Bachelors have to waste a lot of food, like milk and eggs if they have no fridge. It's no use telling me that your mother never had a fridge. She would have cooked fresh every day, but you are going to heat and reheat meals and where can you store fresh food in a wee flat?"

She sold me the fridge and a very smart [well, very clean] cream enamel second-hand cooker with four gas rings and a large oven. To top it all, she arranged for me to pay for the lot, including fitting and delivery, on a series of small monthly payments. The appliances, she said would be installed by the Scottish Gas Board's fitters in two days. And it was.

My kitchen, small and tight was almost ready for survival cooking. It had a set of three shelves suitable for storing plates and pans, but it still lacked a work surface for preparing food. By necessity, the world of DIY [do it yourself] dragged me into its tool shop and small white wood furniture store at the corner of Lady Lawson Street. This cheap rough wooden furniture has long ago been replaced by the wonders of IKEA and built-in kitchens, but in 1960, it was exactly what I needed. It also gave me a practical lesson in the storage of potatoes: they quickly pick up the flavour of freshly painted white wood drawers and have to be thrown away.

A kind and understanding Edinburgh City Council in 1960 was running a scheme to help people living in old-fashioned houses, such as mine, to upgrade their property. There was financial assistance to rewire an accommodation and to install a 13 amp circuit mains supply of electricity. I needed that.

There was financial assistance to help install a bathroom with a source of running hot water [not another banger, but a copper tank with an immersion heater]. I needed that.

With the expert help of a genial plumber, Duncan Anderson, who knew his way through the terms and conditions of this scheme, my request was given shape by a young architect, piloted into the Planning Application committee and then steered into the Dean of Guild Court. At the end of four or five months, the application succeeded and a generous grant of 50 % was approved. On top of this, I was allowed to pay my share of the cost in monthly instalments. The whole business had occupied the winter and spring, so the actual work was scheduled for July or August when the house would be empty. Weddings and honeymoons would take centre stage for the summer. We would be elsewhere, but where?

Honeymoon in Berlin

At this point, with only a few weeks of June left, my Godfather in Berlin came to the rescue with a most useful and generous wedding present. He offered us the full use of his luxurious flat in central Berlin for three weeks while he took his own holiday in Madiera. A quick check with Esme Walker in Crichton Street found us a cheap student flight to Berlin from Gatwick. Well, actually, two flights: first from Gatwick to Dusseldorf and then, after a two-hour break, from Dusseldorf to Berlin. Easy peasy lemon squeezy. Nothing could go wrong.

How to Cope with a Crisis and Love the Russians

My future wife was a spinster of the parish of St John, a delightful country church in the village of Keele, standing at the gates of an old Ducal estate [lately the property of a Russian royal prince]. Within its acres of parkland and farms, there rose a magnificent residence, once a veritable small palace, diminutively called 'a hunting lodge' in Russian, but now the administrative centre of the new 'red brick' University of Keele.

Having observed the usual formalities of a Church of England wedding and eaten a lavish meal at the 'Wheat Sheaf' in Onnerly, we bade a ceremonial farewell to friends and family. Borrowing my father's car, we set off for Bakewell in the comfortable heart of Derbyshire. We then spent a few days in Henley on the Thames before presenting ourselves at the Channel Island Airline reception desk in Gatwick.

To our distress, we found that our flight to Berlin with Channel Island Airways had been cancelled at the last minute and would be held over until eight the next morning.

Gatwick Airport in those days was a bit of a country bumpkin relation of Heathrow, some people still think of it in unflattering terms. In 1961, Gatwick closed for the night around 10 pm and there was no question of camping on the floor, so we set off to the bright lights of Crawley. The very name Crawley induces a feeling of aversion, as to some loathsome creature creeping across the floor. There was a hotel room available in a reasonable-looking place, but they had finished serving dinner.

Nothing daunted, the newlyweds walked around the centre of this small town and finding no alternative, we had fish and chips wrapped up in the local newspaper. I thought of keeping this scrap of paper as a honeymoon souvenir, but it smelled of vinegar and fish, so it went into a waste bin at the bus stop. It was still there the next morning when we took the bus back to the airport.

From the hotel, I rang my Godfather in Berlin to report this delay. It was an expensive call because it had to be done through the phone at the hotel reception as, despite the presence of a GPO coin box, I did not have enough small change to be sure of getting through on a long-distance international call. My uncle was not pleased and proposed to set off for Madeira the next morning at eight come or come not who may. We could take a taxi form Tempelhof to Clausewitz Strasse.

Eventually, at about eleven in the morning, a Channel Island Airways plane presented itself for boarding and after a long pause for the various flight regulation formalities, we took off. The journey was long, broken and tedious.

Crisis

We had no inkling of a major international crisis involving Berlin. Had we been better informed of the thousands of East Germans who were abandoning everything to flee to West Germany through the open trapdoor of Berlin, perhaps we would have cancelled our visit to Berlin. As it turned out, we were about to play a small part in history, in an AMFU of huge proportions and even then, I managed to add my own significant contribution to the black comedy.

The divided city of Berlin partitioned between Russia, France, the USA and the UK, was an anomaly, or rather, a political island, surrounded by a sea of Russian-controlled territory. As a result of a wartime compromise, Russia won control of most East European states and half of Germany, but the enemy capital, Berlin, was to be shared between all four in token of their wartime alliance. Adhering strictly to protocol, the Russians allowed their three former Allies direct access [for military personnel only] through one autobahn highway, one rail route and one air corridor. The Russians had already, in 1948, demonstrated their military ability to strangle the road and rail routes, while the Allies had demonstrated their wealth and air power by flying coal trucks into Tempelhof airfield.

Maybe the Western politicians in their summer dreams expected a rerun of the Berlin Airlift. They certainly did not propose to pour men and tanks into an encircled city for a direct military confrontation in which the Russians were overwhelmingly superior and in a winning position. There would be only disaster in reinforcing an untenable position. The Russians certainly would not allow such materiel through their barriers on road and rail access. Had they really wanted to push matters to the limit, they could have closed the air corridor. The unwritten, unspoken rules of the Cold War game, however, required both sides to avoid applying the red heat of force.

Airlift

We knew nothing, but the civil airlines of the world knew that the US Government was subsidising airfares for the flood of people pouring out of East Germany. The US Government was, in fact, flying as many refugees as possible out of Berlin to other parts of West Germany. To do so, they would be paying very generously for all and any plane seats. West Berlin was surrounded by hostile, i.e., East German, territory. Those fleeing their home country, the same East German Democratic Republic, dare not pass by land for fear of being arrested at any frontier. It was immediately apparent that West Berlin with its air corridor was the only route open to East Germans who wanted to enter West Germany. Western governments were rather slow to wake up to the fact that self-preservation would force the Russians or East Germans simply to seal off their portion of the divided city of Berlin. This they duly did by building a wall, but they waited until our honeymoon was nearly over.

The Channel Island Airlines probably shunted aside as many as possible of their economy charter flights in order to cash in on this lucrative opportunity. By the end of our holiday, they had gone out of business and I had to blow what was left of my savings on two BEA tickets to London. There was, therefore, not enough cash left to buy the one piece of household equipment that we lacked: a washing machine. We would be back to the Bendix laundrette and bagwash.

Honeymoon in Berlin, 1961, Cousin Willi

Berlin in the summer of 1961 is a delightful memory, coloured, highlighted and made all the more enjoyable by the presence of my cousin Willi. I had met him first in 1951 when he was a carefree young man, accompanying his father, my godfather, on a Christmas visit to our home in Stoke on Trent. Just four years older than me, he was a carefree bachelor, a trainee in his father's business of supplying the fashion houses of Berlin and West Germany with lace and tulle, buttons and bows, silks and satins, braids and interlinings; in fact, everything that the garment makers could need or use. It seemed a frail business to me, a smokestack industrial apprentice, but it endured and prospered, leaving Willi a well-to-do pensioner at the end of the century.

As a boy of fifteen, Willi had been conscripted into the Wehrmacht and had fought in the siege of Berlin in the anti-tank [panzer nakow] brigade. He told us quite amazing stories of narrow escapes and daring subterfuges. Eventually, he had been rounded up into a Russian POW camp and, as a young squirt, had been delegated to the most unpleasant work: 'the shit house commando'. Squalid and overcrowded, the prison camp, with its primitive open-air latrines was literally a cess pool of infection. Inevitably, he had contracted infectious hepatitis and become too weak and too sick to work. The Russians thought that he was not worth transporting to Siberia with the bulk of prisoners of war, so they just threw him out into the street. Yellow as a canary, and surrounded by refugees in utter confusion, Willi scrambled onto the roof of an overloaded train and made his way back to Berlin.

Clausewitz Strasse

Willi and my godfather lived in a large flat at 3 Clausewitz Strasse, just off the Kurfurstendam. This tall six-storey apartment building belonged to the early nineteen hundreds and so had its own passenger lift, the very latest convenience. Grand pianos, however, as we saw one morning, still had to be hoisted up a gigantic telescopic ladder affair that belonged to the furniture removers. The size of this contraption served to explain the tall oval passage that opened the inner courtyard of this group of apartment buildings.

From our bedroom window, we could look down into this courtyard with its grassy lawn and bushy birch tree. There was a pleasant acoustic to this arena and it was used to great effect by singers who would come, mainly on a Sunday, to deliver an aria and collect a few coins.

Despite the street's warlike name, it was the very essence of the quiet inner city. The flat was very comfortable and we newlyweds lived in luxury. Every morning at breakfast time, a pleasant housekeeper turned up to clean the place and to do the laundry. Frau Imke, however, had a problem. Each day she travelled in from the eastern part of Berlin because the value of the Deutchmarks that Willi paid her for housework bought far more than the East German marks earned by her husband for driving trains. She desperately wanted to flee to the west, but her husband refused to abandon his state railway pension.

Less than half aware of the gravity of the situation, which seemed to be just a little local difficulty, we newlyweds walked along the warm, sunny Kurfurstendam. This broad busy boulevard with trams on either side of a broad grassy centre, itself dotted with kiosks and eating places, was then at the heart of West Berlin. Everything seemed so normal, so carefree with everyone so relaxed and there seemed to be nothing to spoil the holiday mood. We looked at expensive things laid out in elaborate shop window displays and marvelled at the luxurious furnishings and wonderful foods displayed in KDW, the Berlin equivalent of London's Harrods.

Entry into East Berlin was easy enough, requiring only the production of 'dokumenten', in our case a passport. It all seemed everyday and normal. Even in East Berlin, there was no need for us to worry or to feel threatened.

The giant portals of the Brandenburg Gate stood open to traffic, guarded by a carefully preserved Soviet tank that had fought in the final battle for the German capital. This sealed grey relic was itself guarded day and night by a Red Army honour guard, the changing of which was a tourist attraction on a scale comparable with Buckingham Palace. Once a day, the soldiers left their stone guardhouse, a cottage built in classic style beside the gate. Every day, the Soviets reminded the world that victory was theirs and that they had paid for it in millions of deaths.

To drive home their point, they erected a statue of a Red Army soldier in Soviet heroic style and they built it fifty metres tall. It could be neither ignored nor hidden. We wanted to see this giant.

Once through the gate, we were careful to point out that we carried a camera and to enquire about the protocol for its use by tourists. The policeman who ushered us through seemed surprised at our query. "Take photos everywhere: we are proud of what we have built," he said.

We walked, accordingly, through the very centre of the rebuilt city, viewing the Protestant Cathedral and the restored Museum Island with its bullet pockmarks around all the lower windows. Inside the museum was rather stark, forcing the visitor to concentrate on the glazed tiles cladding the remains of one of the city wall gates of Babylon. The British Museum would have had at least one gift shop selling souvenirs and reproductions, but the customers of the Pergamon were treated as just a nuisance. Who on earth would buy a fragment of glazed brick or a lump of stone in a Berlin museum as a souvenir of a Byzantine wall? The answer came nearly thirty years later.

Unter den Linden, the boulevard of Bismark and the Kaisers was a terrible disappointment, lying in the eastern half, stripped of all former grand associations and disfigured by what Willi called 'Wedding Cake' architecture in the Soviet style. Massive pink and white apartment blocks lined the street, forming a district of exclusive flats for the Nomenclature, the bigwigs of the Communist Party.

It was forced upon us that East and West Berlin were being used as two massive showcases competing for customers on behalf of two different political systems. Both sides had some quite spectacular new buildings, and both sides had achieved some beautiful restorations, yet the competition remained weighted towards the west. In 1961, the East Germans were giving their verdict by voting with their feet.

In the Tiergarten, the equivalent of Hyde Park, there stood the results of a competition in modern architecture. Looking out onto the great grassy lawns on one side and backed by the broad belt of trees that flanked the River Spree, a small complex of high-rise and single-storey homes winked their windows in the sun and spread their newly painted white walls. Nothing like this was to be found in Stoke on Trent, nor even in Scotland, where city councils endlessly stamped out cheap versions of Soviet workers' high-rise flats. I had toured the Castlemilk estate, built in the fifties to rehouse central Glasgow's 'overspill' from the slums of Gorbals and such places. Glasgow's attempt at Soviet modernity did not even compete with these Scandinavian buildings in the Tiergarten.

West Berlin was making vigorous efforts to repair its many war-ruined buildings and making tentative efforts to restore interrupted lines of communication within the city. Of these, the most important one and the one best restored was the Underground [U-Bahn], linking with the Suburban railway [S-Bahn]. There were identity card checks on crossing the arbitrary zonal divisions, but at least communication existed. There was a guarded optimism that things would get better; that the West Berlin showcase city would slowly convince the East Germans that the good life was possible also for them.

Even the local VW dealer made an entertaining contribution to the showcase liveliness of the Kurfurstendam with his service centre. By putting the cars for routine servicing on a moving conveyor, about 100m long, running the length of a side street. The proud owner could view through a series of large showroom windows each and every stage of the service. It would take 30 minutes precisely.

For all this, there was good reason to dismiss the East German haemorrhage of people as just a summer holiday event.

Borsch

Most evenings, Willi would take us out to a cosy, but inexpensive eating place. One night in particular was memorable because we went to an eating place in a large wooden hut beside a lake [Berlin is surrounded by lakes and rivers]. There we had a large tureen of Borsch soup that was so good that we ordered a second tureen. It was only on our way back that Willi mentioned that we had been in the Russian sector, for Berlin was still divided among the occupying powers. He was right to mention it late rather than earlier; he might have spoiled our appetite.

Nevertheless, apart from the guards at the Brandenburg Gate, the Russian troops were invisible. The East German police, almost indistinguishable from their soldiers, were in charge of the daily running of the city. On the streets, there was absolutely nothing to disturb the visitor lazily wandering through the warm summer boulevards.

Willi was a most thoughtful host who introduced us to his wide circle of friends, most of whom were of our own age, in their late twenties and early thirties. There was a scarcely concealed sadness among the young Germans that we met. They were very pessimistic about the future, mainly in terms of the Cold War and nuclear weapons. Seeing that we were newly married, they spoke to us very directly about their pessimism about the future and their own reluctance to have children who would be fed straight into an army mincing machine.

Most of Willi's contemporaries, men who had served briefly as boy soldiers still retained visions of air raid shelters and bombed streets filled with tanks and soldiers. With other, more recent memories of how the US and Britain had stood aside while the Russians invaded Hungary, their gloom seemed fully justified. Certainly, the Russians could have snuffed out the other garrison armies in Berlin within hours and this fact made the confrontation between them both more ridiculous and more serious. The young adults with whom we shared meals or drinks or strolls in the park spoke nothing about the wartime experiences that they all shared. They had had their fill of horrors; heroics held neither meaning nor attraction. Their longing for a 'normal' peaceful life was probably reciprocated by the thousands fleeing East Germany with its paranoid culture of surveillance and suspicion.

Willi, by contrast, was a carefree bachelor who had been brought to the brink of an early death during the siege of Berlin and who, as a result, never worried about anything. He had a different girlfriend whenever we went out, which we did regularly. There was, however, one who was so special that we were never allowed to meet her; in fact, he particularly requested our absence from the apartment on two evenings. The task of entertaining ourselves in this lively city was anything but arduous, but it did involve me in yet another mistake. I'll confess in full later.

Over the later years of Willi's life, there were various affairs that seemed to promise marriage, but he never quite brought a bride to the altar. Perhaps, after a certain point in life, some people simply are so deeply committed to their own privacy that sharing becomes impossible. On casual acquaintance, Willi seemed a selfish hedonist, but he was, in fact, one of the most generous people on earth. His tastes were simple [as Oscar Wilde wrote], he simply liked the best of everything. Tea, cheese and ham for breakfast came from KDW and that was also the source of his whisky, a 15-year-old Macallan malt.

He had no religious conviction: he showed no interest in such things, unlike his father, Heinz, who remained a borderline Christian all his life and who celebrated Christmas 1970 by taking his sister [my mother] to visit Bethlehem.

Willi seemed a simple soul, but of course, was far from it. He had a passion for the great German composers, mainly Bach, Haydn and Brahms, whose music filled his breakfast hour. A man of fixed habits, as you might already have guessed, Willi liked to have his English breakfast tea brewed exactly to the second in a red clay teapot. His housekeeper looked after everything else, cleaning floors, ironing shirts: in short, acting as a mother. Their relationship was to last sixty years.

A City Under Siege

Meantime, isolated from BBC News and newspapers, we continued to explore the delights of Berlin. We swam and sunbathed on a sandy beach by a large lake. We explored museums to find the image of Nefertiti, the wall of Babylonian tiles and the relics of Troy. We found ourselves in the newly restored Rococo beauty of Charlottenburg Palace with its splendid Amber Room. We walked up to the Brandenburg Gate, flanked by a Russian tank and a Russian guard house. This all changed ten days later.

Entertaining ourselves on a summer evening, we two newlyweds decided to go for a drink in 'The Berliner Kindle', a large, affordable and busy restaurant at the top of the Kurfurstendam. We had promised to arrive back at Willi's flat no earlier than 10.30 and decided that a light meal would help our drinks to go down. German menus have always given me trouble when written in Gothic print, but this one was written in clear standard print and had a special section on omelettes. This seemed a reasonable light meal to take in the late evening, but the choice was bafflingly wide. Compromising, we chose 'omelette surprise', feeling that we might discover something special. We did.

This was a very large dining room, about the size of a rugby pitch and our order seemed to take forever to arrive. There was, however, something special going on at the other end of this restaurant. It was not possible to see just what was going on: perhaps some obstreperous person was being troublesome, but whatever was going on was attracting a running wave of attention. From this loose scrum, there appeared a waiter holding aloft a large silver tray laden with some large white object, probably a chicken. He was certainly weaving around, making a great show of this silver salver. He was probably looking for the table that had ordered this huge, showy meal and he was taking his time.

It was a large dining room and although he was circling and moving in waltz time, this waiter was heading straight for us. Desperately looking around at the nearby tables to find which one could possibly have ordered such a monster, we knew it was not ours: we were only having an omelette. Like a descending V2 rocket that dish landed on our table. The surprise was ours and we had, to our amazement ordered a baked Alaska—in other words, a slab of ice cream surrounded by meringue.

The thing was huge, far more than enough for ten people. The waiter joined in the general laughter and, at our request, offered helpings of baked Alaska around the various tables nearby. There was general merriment at my latest goof-up and it didn't cost too much money, but it certainly cost me a lot of self-esteem. Perhaps my wife noticed.

Willi introduced us to the tennis/skating club, where British officers' families could swim in the outdoor pool or play tennis or just relax on the sunny grass. It was here that we first learned of the construction of a wall. Among these service families, there seemed to be no alarm; perhaps they assumed that they would be evacuated before the commencement of hostilities. There was a worrying similarity to the optimism of the garrison of Singapore in 1941, but who could blame these families for enjoying the sunny afternoons and their privileged position as representatives of the occupying powers?

Waiters in smart white short jackets carried trays of tea and cake out onto the great lawn; children ran about licking ice cream cones; everything seemed absolutely normal.

Problems

Against such a threatening background, it was comforting to know that our return flight was only three days away. Full of confidence as an experienced tourist guide, I rang to confirm this flight, as was normal in those days. Channel Islands Airways' desk at Templehof Airport, responded with horror. This flight had left three days earlier, due to an emergency. The company had contacted as many passengers as possible and they were very sorry that some people had been left behind.

Another Cockup Posing as
Heroic Failure

This was my ultimate boob; my Cockup of Imperial Grand Stature [CIGS—no disrespect meant to the late Chief of the Imperial General Staff]. This one could have life-threatening consequences: it was far more serious than a few cardboard lunch boxes.

I kicked myself. I had forgotten that German and Austrian police demanded that all foreigners should register with them within twelve hours of arrival. Oh, hell! If only I had remembered to think like a tourist courier, instead of behaving as a tourist, we would have registered with the police, and our address at Clausewitz Strasse would have been used to warn us of the early departure panic.

Another charter flight was held out as a possibility in a few days' time, but there was no certainty. We were advised to keep in touch; there was no other choice.

Tempelhof may have been West Berlin's lifeline during the 1947/8 airlift, but something more substantial than a promise was needed to transform it into our escape route. After waiting over the weekend, we went to Thos. Cooke on the Kurfurstendam and booked two tickets to London with BEA [British European Airways]. This was money that we had set aside for the purchase of a washing machine, so this represented my cash fine for yet another cockup.

Heinz, my godfather, returned from his holiday and was surprised to find Judy and me still in possession of his bedroom. He put a good face on it and took us out for dinner at a swanky rooftop restaurant in the centre of the city to celebrate our wedding. There the bright lights flashed off silver cutlery and cut glass, while the bourgeoisie of the besieged city laughed and dined as though everything was normal. But it wasn't normal and this was emphasised for all Berlin that evening by a huge explosion that shook the building where we genteelly supped soup. This savage demonstration of unrestrained power rattled the glass of the great panoramic windows.

Only luck or some Russian miscalculation prevented this mighty explosion from shattering the huge glass windows into a thousand deadly flying shards. From our rooftop position, through these still intact windows, we could see a huge cloud of dust, yellow and pink in the ruddy twilight. The word spread around the dining room that the Russians had just demolished a block of apartments that straddled the demarcation line between their sector and the American sector. It was in their way and they did not give a damn for normal civilised behaviour.

For light reading, we had brought along a paperback edition of Arnold Bennett's *Old Wives Tale* and had been sharing it as we lay idly in the warm summer afternoon sun. There are scenes in the novel of the siege of Paris during the 1870 Franco-Prussian war. One particularly vivid episode deals with the use of a gas-filled balloon by the French Army to take people and despatches in and out of the encircled city.

Rambling rather despondently down the Kurfurstendam after purchasing our escape tickets, we noticed some colourful reproduction prints of early flights in balloons. They reflected our longing to escape Berlin by air and so, with our few remaining Deutchmarks, we bought four of them. These were the very first prints to decorate the walls of our home in Well Court, reminding us of the part of our honeymoon that nearly turned into a disaster.

Home and a Conclusion

It was not possible to fly directly from Berlin to Edinburgh, or indeed, to anywhere other than Frankfort or Dusseldorf. This again harked back to the wartime bargain with the Russians. We flew to London and caught a train to Stoke to spend a few days with our respective new in-laws. The tensions and anxiety of our last few days in Berlin were discarded as casually as a soiled operating gown. We were absolutely unaware of having had a very minor role in a major historical event: we had simply suffered some inconvenience and thought no more of it as we returned to our more immediate normality.

In Stoke, it was 'Waikes Week' and most of the town was away at the seaside. Wedding presents were bundled up and sent with Pickfords, the removal firm, to our new home in Dean Village. Among these items, given by an elderly relative was a large box of Havana cigars of goodness only knows what date. I tucked a couple of these delightfully aromatic tokens of luxury into my jacket's top pocket as we set off for a night's visit to the Waikes fair.

For those who have never tried smoking a Havana cigar while riding on a fairground roller coaster, my considered opinion is that it is a boastful display that will end in disaster, as it did for me. I realised the full meaning of the North country expression: 'proper poorly'.

A few days later, my wife and I took the train from Crewe to Edinburgh. Riding through the purple, green and gold heather and bracken-clad hills of the Border country, I suddenly felt that curious rush of emotion that accompanies homecoming.

The plumbers and builders had done their work while we were away. There was a bathroom, constructed by pinching off a section of the living room. The flat had been rewired and the old coal fireplace bricked off and plastered. Duncan Anderson, the man in charge of the development had warned me against doing any decorating before the electricians, plumbers, plasterers and builders had finished. He was right. The whole flat was covered in fine dust. The tradesmen had cleaned up sacks full of brick and plaster, timber cut-offs and odd bits of copper tubing, all the unconsidered trifles of major refurbishment.

What we had to do was to buy mops and brushes, buckets and pails, soaps and cleaning items. We went up to Greys the Ironmonger on George Street and opened a monthly account that actually gave us about six weeks of credit. We loaded our many purchases onto a sturdy five-foot wooden stepladder, which, for those who may be interested, is still available to view in our garage.

The Potteries seemed long ago and far away from my home in Edinburgh, which now folded me back into its comfortable embrace. I was like a child with a new toy: I was impatient to show my wife whatever I knew about Scotland, this mist-wrapped, beautiful country of hills and waters.

There would be no more guided tours; future travels would be for family and friends only. Jock Peggie, that impresario of the touring bus, understood immediately. Each year, he toured more or less the same venues and every two or three years or so, the main actors would change. The storyline, however, did not vary; as for the audience, it changed twice a day and resembled sea-washed pebbles on a beach, with both an individual identity and a common character. Jock Peggie would go on for years, but the show goes on forever.

As for me, my feet of Potteries clay had taken root in the tangled heather of Scotland. My wife and I were about to start a family of little Scots.